DEDICATED TO

My mother Dr. Sarojini Ramarao
on her eightieth birthday!
Thank you Amma, for everything.

Contents

Preface

This book is about you.
This book is about your emotions.
This book is about your emotional intelligence.

At the same time it is important to acknowledge that intelligence and its academic attributes play a large role in a person's success. This cannot and should not be ignored.

However it has time and again been found that there is a something, which makes a less intelligent person successful and hinders a well-qualified person from making it to the top.

And this is Emotional Intelligence.

The theme of this book is:

To learn to be aware of all your emotions.

To exercise control over your emotions and learn to use them appropriately.

To help you use these skills to make a success of your life.

And to emphasize that each person's reactions to his particular problem are different. There are very few common denominators.

And the final choice is yours.

You are the architect of your life.

This book is positive; its emphasis is in making you aware, so that you have added EQ to your repertoire of IQ to make you a complete and happy person.

Jyotsna Codaty

PS. In this book, the word 'man' is used to mean the species of man, in both the genders.

I

The Beginning

Once upon a time, there was a man. He studied well and got a good job. He got up in the morning, went to work and came home in the evening to spend time with his family. They all sat around talking about their day's work, ate meal together, went to sleep. Festivals were great occasions for togetherness with the entire family of aunts and uncles and their children coming together. Somehow, life went on at an even pace. They read stories about the great people of earlier decades who went to study abroad, but were willing to give up their riches and highly remunerative careers to come back and serve in their own country. Then there were others who were also prepared for a long stay in the jail. These great freedom fighters motivated men to think on higher plane than the usual business talk.

In a few decades things changed. Nobody knew how, or why, or even when, but slowly life became a big race and it became essential that one got some sort of a ranking in that race. There was a race to admit children in schools, there was a race to drive the best car, there was a race to be seen in the best restaurants and holiday spots, there was a race to spend more and more on one's child's birthday or wedding. And there was even a race as to ensure one's heart surgery was more expensive than others. Man got caught up in this rat race. It appeared that if he was not participating in this race, he was an outsider in society. Winning was all that mattered—by hook or crook. In short, the end justified the means!

Again there was a change. Man decided that there was something lacking in this lifestyle. Highly educated that he was, he asked scientists the answer. Sure enough, they came up with the solution. Man was not using his emotions enough! To qualify and quantify these emotions, they came up with theories and tools. And that is how the concept of Emotional Intelligence was born in today's world.

In this period of transition from a purely intelligence-based judgment to an intelligent and emotion-based one, man somewhere along the way got confused. He was used to applying his mind, and today they say, he must use his heart too! Sometimes he feels he is like a computer—where data is fed in, and the answer comes out from his mind. Where is the person in me, he asks himself. Why am I not looking beyond the data in front of me? Am I missing out on something? His mind is in a turmoil; he is unable to understand his emotions. At such times, he stands near the sea and gazes into the deep blue waters.

The blue waters of the sea touching the shoreline with gentle waves are one of the most beautiful sights of Nature. They bestow a sense of calmness in those who watch it from far. The vastness of the blue waters seem to imperceptibly join the blue skies, each reflecting the colours of the other. The gentle waves lap at your feet, wash them and then vanish again to mingle with the deep waters. They seem to take you a little distance with them, into the depths of their inner self. The wavy patterns they leave behind on the sand are little designs left on the earth for your pleasure. The shore is dotted with the wealth it has left behind a little present for you. And as you wait, there comes another wave, and there is no telling from a distance whether it is a massive one that will drench you totally and take you deeper than you expect it to, or on the way to the shore it may will sober down to a gentle caress. Anyway, it will bring you some more gifts. Sometimes, it may be seashells to play with or a jellyfish. Other times, it could bring you debris from the bottom of the ocean, and then what will you do with it? Throw it back into the sea, wash your hands in the waters that surround you and get along with your life, or moan at your luck for the unwelcome debris that has come your way?

Perhaps nothing describes emotions better than the waves of the sea. There is just no stopping them, for they roll in one after another, seemingly effortlessly, totally unpredictable in their power and strength, and with the unwavering capacity to draw you along. Perhaps the only constant here is that *they will come*—'*when*' and '*where*' again are imponderables. In the last minute, the waves may change direction, or the winds and the depths of the sea may lessen their ferocity. The vastness of the experience or the ease with which they pass over remains to be seen.

But why talk of emotions? We know that we laugh when we are happy, and cry when we are sad. We are angry or sad when things don't happen the way we want them to, and are pleased when things go our way. So what has all of this got to do with life? Something happens, and we react; it all depends on '*what*' happens to us.

Not really. Man has been conditioned to gloss over emotions. "Emotions are an unfortunate happening—not all are something to look forward to, and some at best are tolerated, preferably in private. Emotions we have been told, interfere with our work; prevent us from taking rational decisions, and should never be permitted to encroach upon our professional lives." And with this predominant mindset, some decades have passed. In fact, 'passed us over,' would be the correct thing to say—for this attitude has left us bereft of some finer feelings in life. Possibly richer in terms of intelligence; intelligence gained by the sheer virtue of extra time stolen away from our emotions—to one of cramming inert data.

And suddenly like the anomaly of the sea with its continuous waves, another wave has come upon us. This time, one that tells us that it is very important for us to be in constant touch with our emotions, to feel each feeling deeply and to appreciate the sensations it causes in us; so that we can understand the feelings of another individual in identical situations, so that we can feel one with him, thereby helping him to cope better. And in the whole process, the entire sequel of identifying with one's own feelings and then being in rapport with those of others, one is enriched!

And the new magical word is EIQ – Emotional Intelligence Quotient. The last couple of decades have passed by with an accent on IQ or the Intelligence Quotient, the so called quantifying element of a person's intelligence. Various tests have been used for this purpose, and the resultant figures attached as labels to a person. One was automatically 'slotted.' And since these quantifying tests were constantly happening consciously or unconsciously to people at various levels—from early school days to middle years in the job market—a person tended to have this label attached to him on a permanent basis. This was often a deterrent even when it was favourable, for it forced him into situations that he could have well done without. Imagine the winner of medals at a young age—even before he leaves school. He is a medalist, and has to keep on winning medals! You can imagine the havoc it creates among people bestowed with an unfavourable tag.

That is not to say that one can well do without any intelligence or the power of sheer knowledge. Facts are facts, and there are many situations in life where it is imperative to have your facts right.

However, the wheel having turned full circle, there is equal emphasis at the emotional level—of what is commonly called, gut instinct, street smartness; I prefer to call it a certain "sensitivity." This positive quality, in the language that is much in vogue today is Emotional Intelligence.

With decades of experience of doing without it, man has come to the conclusion that there is something missing in his life. That something which helps him to function better in all spheres of life, from his career to his personal life; that can help a kid, and can equally help an elderly man, in making a decision. And to acquire that something, one does not need to cram any more text books or answer difficult viva-voce examinations, but rely on a sound gut feeling; something that ought to come naturally to him but has been curtailed and restricted by decades of teaching and conditioning.

It is time now to unshackle ourselves from the constraining bonds of "intelligence only matters, everything else is a waste" as grasped from learning hard facts, to let it encompass finer feelings of life with all its emotions.

When I was one and twenty
I heard a wise man say:
"Give crowns and pennies and guineas
But not your heart away."

No, don't give your heart away, but think with your heart, for the heart feels!

•••

II

Are you Emotionally Literate?

Knowledge is two-fold and consists not only in an affirmation of what is true, but also in the negation of that which is false.

Charles Caleb Cotton

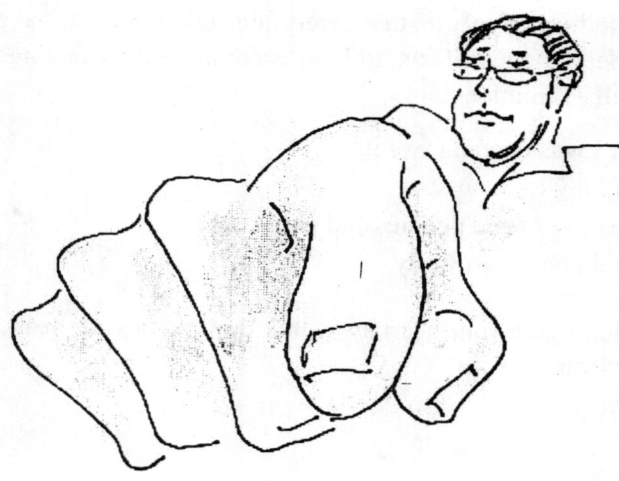

Before the child can actually lisp out words like Mama and Papa, the proud parents begin planning and plotting various courses for their little one. The Alphabet in all its twenty-six lettered glory, both in capitals and lower case with the picture books that go hand in hand to illustrate the marvellous story of the word, are brought home. After that, for all days to come, the parents are pushing the child to achieve better. The Olympian motto could not have better aspirants!

So the three R's are taken care of, and academic proficiency hopefully assured – and the parent lives with his fantasy that all is going to be well in his child's life. The IQ build up is well catered to with sufficient inputs at all levels. Some may also make it to a MENSA score. But is it a firm guarantee that it will make him a success in his career? All of us have heard this story in most families about how so and so's son won all the gold medals in college, but was not doing really well in his career; on the contrary, we also hear of that rather dumb boy in college on whom none placed their bets to have done fairly well for himself in later years. Will the academic background assure that the child grows up into a well-adjusted man who can handle all the issues that keep cropping up in life? In short, to cope with life itself? Are you emotionally literate?

How do you assess a person's skills in this department? There are unfortunately no classes, and definitely no exams. So what is the final score going to be like? In a society that puts heavy emphasis on marks and ranks, and has taken to accepting short cuts like coaching classes in its stride as a marker of the dictum, "the end justifies the means," what parameters are we going to use to quantify the accomplishments in this field? Worse, there are no medals to acquire, no badges to display, no merit cards to boast of. When there is no tangible benefit, no visible accolade, how are you even sure you have acquired this skill? Simple.

Your inner happiness and contentment will come through.
You will be at peace with yourself.

This is not to make light the pursuit of academics either for themselves or as a means of making a good career. Far from it. What is being highlighted is that while a good academic background is important, it is not essentially a guarantee for a successful career. If it were so, then how would one explain this dichotomy of the not-so-good student making a name for himself, and the medallist failing to do so? It cannot easily be explained away as the exception to the rule, for research in this field is slowly but surely proving it to be the rule itself. This takes us to the evolvement of a new mindset—Emotional Intelligence commonly called EQ or Emotional Quotient—but really is EIQ or Emotional Intelligence Quotient. In the succeeding pages, we will restrict ourselves to the use of the word EQ, for that is the popular name.

Welcome to the new era of enlightenment.

How is EQ or for that matter IQ measured?

IQ is measured by standard tests that have been in vogue for a long time. EQ, on the other hand is the new kid on the block, tests that exist for the purpose are few and much contested.

A small questionnaire to highlight the disparities between IQ and EQ.

Have:	IQ	EQ
1. Definite hierarchical structure	Yes	No
2. A step system with blocks	Yes	No
3. Performance rewards like medals	Yes	No
4. Check system for quality assurance	Yes	No
5. Assurance of entry in job market	Yes	No
6. Guarantees for sustained growth	Yes	Yes
7. Specified training programmes	Yes	No
8. Self help tests	Yes	Yes
9. Special teachers	Yes	No
10. Life-long training sessions	No	Yes

In short, there does not seem to be much going in favour of EQ. The scales seem heavily loaded on the side of IQ, which is popular to this day. For sure, academic achievements are not going to move out of fashion fast.

But it has been proven over and over again that the person with the high IQ is not necessarily the one who is doing well in life.

There is some exclusive quality that differentiates men in using an attribute that seems to be scoring over IQ.

This wonder quality is called Emotional Intelligence.

The measure of this quality is called EIQ, or Emotional Intelligence Quotient.

The shorter and catchy word is EQ.

To show a simple parallel, the person's brainpower is intelligence, and the measure of the same is called IQ.

Likewise, a person's emotional power is emotional intelligence, sometimes called emotional health, is a quality, and its measure is EQ.

Emotional health and emotional intelligence are interchangeable, though the more catchy word is EQ, again sometimes called Emotional Intelligence Quotient or EIQ. We will, for convenience sake, use EQ in this book.

EQ is holding on to its own, and appears to be catching on fast.

- So where do you go to train in this elusive skill?
- Which teacher will you find to tutor you in EQ?
- And how long will it take to graduate, or in fact do your doctorate in this subject?

The whole world is your classroom.
Anyone and everyone are your teachers.
A lifetime my friend, because you can never stop learning.

The School that Teaches EQ

Life is the big school that teaches EQ. To put it more bluntly, Nature gifted us this skill on a platter right from childhood. It is often said that a two-year old has the finest sense of emotions.

A two-year old registers the following emotions at appropriate times:

1. When he sees his mother	he smiles	happiness/*love*
2. When he is hungry	he cries	need/*sadness*
3. When he is hurt	he cries	pain/*sadness*
4. When he is displeased	throws tantrums	*anger*
5. When he is scared	stops acting/crying	*fear*.

Love, Sadness, Anger and Fear are the predominant emotions in a human being. The rest of them (remember the *nava rasas?*) are derived from these basic emotions. The final outcome, or the net result, is the last one—peace or *'shanti'*.

If a two-year old has all these feelings, what happens to them in later years? Naturally speaking, one would assume that the existing skills were sharpened, fine tuned and put to good use. Unfortunately, that is not the case. Such skills that Nature has bestowed on us have been taken away, erased, deleted by man with meticulous planning. Our social structure and our teaching institutions have planned in a methodical manner to deplete our mind of these emotions, in the belief that, Emotions were acute disturbances of an individual. Or Emotions were disorganized responses which come from a lack of judgment; a complete loss of cerebral control.

Given this mindset, no wonder they methodically went about to wipe emotions away from our mind, face and thought—to the extent, that we started believing that it was a sign of weakness to show emotions!

Raju has just come home from school. He has begun to go to a play-school only recently. In the beginning, he was upset, and would cry a lot, but slowly, he got used to the school set-up, and after two months, is quite eager to go to school and waits for his mother to drop him there. Today, however, his mother Sabita is greeted not by a smiling Raju eager to tell her all that happened in the class, but a tearful Raju, dirty and torn shirt and his face tear-stained. Sabita's heart melts at the sight of her son. She hugs him and asks him what was the matter. Sabita's gesture of affection opens the floodgates in Raju, and he starts sobbing. Words would not come out of his mouth. An anxious Sabita goes to the class and enquires from the school teacher as to what went wrong. The teacher smiles and says that the quarrel started with the other boy breaking Raju's pencil box, and soon, the matter had escalated to a minor war. By the time the teacher intervened, both the boys were at each other, hammer and tongs. Sabita decides to ignore the matter, and consoles Raju saying, "It's okay, wipe your face. We will go and get another pencil box. These things happen in school; you defended your property, and in the process got a little hurt. So you must not get upset about this." Raju is somewhat consoled, but when he meets his grandmother Kamala, he starts crying again. Immediately, grandmother Kamala hugs him and says, "My Raja *beta* should not cry. Wipe your tears. What will *Dadaji* say if he sees you crying? Have you ever seen Daddy or *Dadaji* crying? Men do not cry, and never in public. The boy who hit you must be punished. I will tell *Papa* to speak to your teacher." To console him, she gives him some ice cream and promised him another pencil box.

The first lesson he learnt was never to show his emotions in public, never to cry, never to show that he is hurt; because brave men do not give way to emotions in public. The next lesson he learnt was to put the blame on the other person. Always, YOU are correct—it is the other ones who are at fault.

An older school boy, Rahul, has a test the next day. To score good marks, he has to complete a project. This involved some amount of creativity, as the model of a dam had to be made. He decided to work along with his friend Sachin so that both could pool resources and submit a good project. Although Sachin had little material with him, he was a good artist and his contribution was all the artistry he put into the model. The finished project looked very nice, and both the boys were proud of their handiwork. They happily showed the model to the family. After Sachin left, Rahul's father called him aside and said that he would always find people who would sponge off him in life. That he should be careful of such people who bring little to a project but expect to get fifty percent of the credit. "But papa," Rahul said, "Sachin did all the painting. I am very clumsy with a paint brush, while he paints very nicely." Rahul's father immediately said, "That is exactly what I am telling you. Be careful of people who do not bring much except their hands to a project. And now, he will get as many marks as my son. You must be very careful about not sharing your marks with anyone. It is the last decimal point of the marks that will get you a seat in college."

The second lesson here is the signal from father to the son that marks are of maximum importance, and that other niceties fail in comparison. In short, your own interests come first.

These are very common incidents that one comes across often in life. If you try to recollect such instances, you will find numerous instances of the kind in your life itself. What is the cause and effect of these instances and what is the net result of these reinforced statements?

The parent, trying to make his son the super achiever that he would like him to be, is trying to protect him from all and sundry. He believes that by guiding his son to be a little selfish, he is teaching him to protect his interests, which is not a bad thing at all. He genuinely does not believe that his instructions would do his son any harm. The son has learnt this lesson by repeated inculcation of the same thought time and again by his parents. By the time he grows up, the idea has firmly set in his mind that he has to be a trifle selfish when it comes to things pertaining to his career. He works his way through college with these beliefs. When he gets a good job in a reputed firm, all are happy. But the habits learnt when young were continued. He is always a trifle wary of others.

During the course of his work, he has to work on projects that required inputs from various individuals. There is no question of who scores over whom, but rather a question of good team work.

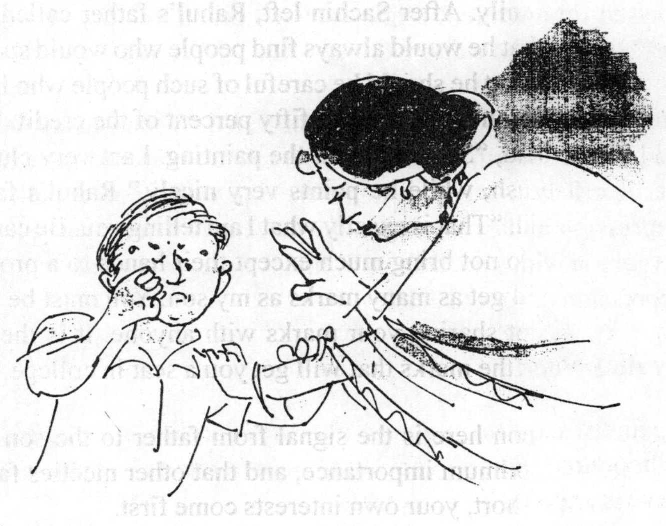

Initially, Rahul is uncomfortable. He grows up with the notion of "take care of yourself first," and was tempted to hide some information and use it for his personal betterment. Fortunately, he quickly learnt that such an attitude would only harm him, and gave in to the tenets of good teamwork.

As an adult, Rahul had to undo the teachings of his childhood to ultimately do well in his job! In fact, the very same reason for which his father was training him!

In the first instance, we saw how the boy was asked to behave like a man! And a man does not cry. It is a sign of weakness to show emotions. Is it? Is it a sign of weakness to cry when you hear some bad news, whether you are a man or woman? Is it a sign of weakness to cry with pain when you are hurt, physically, which is easy to show, and mentally, which is not at all easy to show? Is it a sign of weakness to shed tears of happiness when you are sending away your just married daughter to her home? Is it a sign of weakness to weep for the young soldier who laid down his life for the country? Is it a sign of weakness to cry when you have lost a very important contract that could have done your business a world of good? You must be joking, you are saying to yourself. Cry? When do I lose a contract? Okay, I will feel bad, very bad, I might be depressed for a while, I might even get drunk, but cry? Forget it! Never! It would be a crazy thing to do.

There exactly lies the answer, my dear friend. When you are feeling so bad about something, anything, a few tears would have had a cathartic effect . Instead, you preferred to walk another path, that of depression and/or turning to drink. This is where you will find that a person with a good EQ will find it easier to cry than to give in to depression or turn to drink.

Why do I Need EQ

The gains of acquiring a good university education are tangible and time honoured. Setting goals in terms of the degrees you wish to achieve is universally acceptable.

Where does then EQ figure in the entire scheme of things?
What is it that I will gain in addition by this new skill EQ?
How am I going to lose out if I do not acquire this talent/art/skill?

These are some basic questions that deserve to be answered before one is convinced about the goodness of cultivating EQ. I use the term cultivating in opposition to the words *learn* or *teach* as this is not a skill that can be learnt in five easy lessons, or six months of bi-weekly classes. This is a skill that has to be acquired, cultivated by practice, on yourself and also in your interaction with others.

During the course of long researches in different fields, scientists have observed that something is lacking in all persons. That *'something'* can be nebulously called human interaction, some sort of feeling for others, putting yourself in the shoes of others before making judgments, not being overtly judgmental and so on. Something rings a bell in your mind. I seem to be repeating all the things your grandmother told you while reading "Panchatantra" to you! Only she did not give it a name, but expected a decent human being to behave with what Shakespeare called, "the milk of human kindness."

But what has all this got to do with my job or my career? It has a lot to do with every action of human beings, and can quantitatively increase the responses one gets from the respondent. Now that I have mentioned the word, "gets out of," interest perks up! Because all human interaction has been brought down to a few strategic words.

"What is in it for me?"

"What do I get out of it?"

In short, the benefit to "I" matters more than anything else. The necessity to relearn EQ would not have risen if it was not sacrificed to this "I" phenomenon.

Like they say in various parables, "Ask not what the country can do for you, but ask what you can do for your country." This little line best encapsulates the spirit of EQ when you substitute country with friend, family, neighbour or anyone else.

Let me illustrate with a few examples. Raman was late for a presentation because his assistant was late. He was upset about this, and intended to speak to the consultant about his assistant's wayward behaviour. This is the second time he is late for work this week. Last time, he gave the excuse that his wife was sick and that she had to be taken to the hospital. At about that time, his assistant, Kumar, came panting, and said, "Sorry boss, I am late. Had to take the wife to the doctor again as she had a severe attack of Asthma – could not breathe literally." Raman was very angry, but somehow, controlled his temper and went on with the presentation. His anger caused the first few minutes to be a little patchy, but the veteran that he was, he managed. Still, he felt that the anger in him caused his performance to be below par. Later he had a talk with Kumar to find out what exactly the problem was. He then advised him to take the services of a good specialist and to keep all the medicines at hand; hopefully, hospitalization would be minimized. Also, his wife could attend to her problem promptly even if Kumar was away at work. When all this was done, he assured him that he was always there to help out if needed. Kumar was very happy that he had such an understanding boss. He was more committed to his work for the privilege of working with such an understanding man.

Here we have dealt with a boss, Raman who has a good measure of EQ. He was angry, but he did not shout – that would have been the stereotyped attitude of the person in a commanding position. Actually had he tried some stress-relieving tactic like walking a bit and deep breathing before going into the presentation, he would have fared better. He talked to Kumar about his problem and tried to offer solutions. Thirdly, he reinforced the idea that all of them were there to share his problems, and did not isolate him with a, "I could not care less about your problems. I want the work done, come what may."

Of course, EQ is essential to all cadres. And this to say that somebody like Kumar should not be at the receiving end only, and it is the duty of a senior man to help. In the ideal situation, Kumar should have approached Raman with the problem of his wife's health and sought his help. Of course, this could have been the first few times that his wife fell ill, and he himself was unaware of the situation.

In other words, in another era, this would have been put down as a normal situation and also as what is expected of a person in such circumstances. No special points here for doing what is expected of you as a human being. In his earlier works, a pioneer in this field, Daniel Goleman calls EQ as good old-fashioned "CHARACTER" much to the concern of other scientists. But in today's competitive world, where sensibilities are somewhat restricted to that all encompassing word—competitiveness—a special word needs to be coined, and advertised as the *newage mantra.* Only then does it have an appeal, and that too, I am afraid, for the wrong reasons to score a special point.

In that event, the very purpose is defeated. You notice that the visual media these days focus on qualities that would have been considered *namby–pamby* till a few years ago. The topnotch executive leaves an important board meeting to attend to his little daughters phone call, another executive does not forget to assist an elderly lady at the bus stop, or help a school student to collect funds for a deserving cause. In short, the world is changing, and the idea is being reinforced that there are some simple things in life that are worth doing.

You need not gain anything from it – in fact, you should not expect to gain anything from it. Isn't that what the Bhagawad Gita said?

Perhaps today EQ needs to be studied as a subject in management or even for any and everyone because society as such has become totally materialistic. Totally existentialist. What better way than to say it than in a scientific way, in a way that it challenges the IQ—to eventually make an amalgam of both?

●●●

III

What is Emotional Intelligence?

I *think therefore I am.*
(Cognito, ergo sum)

Descrates, ***Principles of Philosophy.***

Good EQ is all about being able to identify all your emotions, and being able to express them.

Emotion is a *'felt-tendency'* to move towards something assessed as good or favourable and away from something assessed as bad or unfavourable. It is also called a 'feeling'.

Let us examine some statements, and see if in your perception, they are fact or fiction.

1. Emotional health is related to physical health.
2. The most important relationship in life is the relationship with your life partner.
3. If you sometimes feel like a child when you are sad, you are emotionally immature, and it is time when you grow up. The world does not tolerate a weakling.
4. Since you cannot change the past, it is a waste to go into childhood events and examine childhood experiences.
5. People with high self-esteem focus on their positive qualities and do not see their negative attributes.
6. It is best to reject illogical or unpleasant feelings.

First. The answer to this is *True*. Emotional health is a key part of total well being. Most emotionally healthy people take good care of their physical selves. They eat well, exercise and get enough rest. They work to develop supportive personal relationships and are often well developed spiritually. It is related to total well-being.

Second. *False*. The most important relationship in life is the one you have with yourself. To be emotionally healthy, you first need to know yourself. You need to examine your thoughts, needs, values and feelings. You also need to discover the various aspects of your personality and to recognize the stages of life that await you.

Three. *False*. It is absolutely normal to feel like a child when you are sad.

Four. *False*. It is important to examine childhood experiences because the messages received in childhood influence emotional health today.

Five. *False*. People with high self-esteem learn to accept the positive and negative sides of themselves.

Six. *False*. It is best to deal with all feelings as promptly as possible, even those that seem illogical or unpleasant. It is, however, not always in one's best interest to act on them. This should not be confused with acting emotionally. Experiencing your emotions is very different from acting emotionally. In fact, acting emotionally is best avoided. The proper thing to do is to recognize your emotion, accept it, and act after you have worked through your emotion.

Many people claim that our emotional health is so important that it "affects what we do, who we meet, who we marry, how we look, how we feel, the course of our lives and even how long we live."

In short, Emotional Intelligence/Quotient can be said to be:

- Knowing how you and others feel and what to do about it.
- Knowing what feels good and what feels bad and how to move from the bad to the good.
- The emotional awareness, sensitivity and management skills help us to maximize our long-term happiness and survival.

Some components of EI are:

- Being aware of your own emotions as they are occurring.
- Being emotionally literate, that is being able to identify and label various emotions, and also to communicate clearly and directly to others what you feel.
- The ability to make intelligent decisions using a healthy balance of emotion and reason. Being neither too emotional nor too rational.
- The ability to manage and take responsibility for your own emotions, especially the responsibility for self-motivation and personal happiness.

So the whole question of EQ boils down to emotions. Let us look at emotions in some detail.

A sample of emotions and their extremes:

Affection – love
Anger – rage
Dislike – revulsion
Desire – lust

Distress	–	anguish
Excitement	–	frenzy
Fear	–	terror
Happiness	–	ecstasy
Interest	–	fascination
Possessiveness	–	jealousy
Shame	–	humiliation
Sorrow	–	agony.

It is quite natural to feel any of these emotions. However, it may be necessary to suppress an emotion momentarily, as in the case of fear. This is for your own protection, or the very emotion of fear may incapacitate you. But at the earliest moment, one must face the feeling. If it is fear, then one has to go back to the cause and effect reasoning to find out 'why'. And if the situation is inevitable, accept the emotion. Repressed emotions get accumulated and ultimately make it difficult for a person to function in a healthy manner both emotionally and physically. Generally people who are in close touch with their emotions and express them appropriately are emotionally more healthy than people who ignore them.

To verbalize your feelings, express them:

I'm angry   I'm upset

I'm hurt   I'm sad

I'm excited	I'm resentful
I'm envious	I'm anxious
I'm frustrated	I'm afraid
I'm thrilled	I'm stressed
I'm uneasy	I'm touched
I'm nervous	I'm lonely.

Having named your particular feeling and said it aloud, we will go to the next step of tackling it.

How to Tackle Feelings

Yes, feelings are 'those things' that come on to you with a rush. The sort of thing that happens when you cannot but burst out laughing – even when you know it is impolite to do so – or to wipe the tear that is threatening to drop on to your cheeks in a little while.

What can we do about this sudden deluge of feelings? Can we not, rather should we not, keep them in check for a more private or sometimes more appropriate occasion?

I do not believe so. For that is what we have been doing all the while for the last few decades, and somewhere along the way, lost out on 'something'. That *something*, scientific research says is the capacity to feel, the capacity to emote, and consequently, the capacity to feel with others, and to feel for others.

It is time we lifted all the barriers, opened all the floodgates, and let our body in its entirety (mind plus heart) experience all the feelings, totally and fully.

The first step in dealing with feelings is to express them appropriately. That means doing something physical – speaking, writing, crying, shouting, laughing, or otherwise, acting out our emotions.

Let us take the first alternative – speaking. Do question yourself as to how many times in the past two weeks you have made one of the statements expressing your feelings to yourselves or to someone else like, "I am angry today," or "I am happy today." Recognizing these feelings and accepting them as natural is half the battle won. Knowing that you have these feelings can help in dealing with them.

Expressing feelings is sometimes best done physically. Calmly saying, “I am angry,” does not express the feeling. If you speak angrily, it releases more of the emotion. This can be done in private in a closed room; in fact, one can get a little more physical by say, punching a bag when you are angry. The only caveat here is that in getting physical, another person should not be injured by your activity. While punching a pillow is okay, punching or hitting another person is not okay.

Likewise, one can let off steam but yelling, crying, running, dancing or whatever, and then relax to analyze the situation that triggered off the first hostile reaction. This physical activity is a temporary means of dissimulating your anger, and not a solution. The analysis that follows the ‘working off’ of the anger is likely to yield results. This has to be worked out by each individual by himself as no two situations, or the reaction of two human beings to the same situations are ever the same.

Sometimes, the negative feelings keep returning. That is a signal that you need to reassess the situation and maybe, a confrontation is necessary. There is a story of the gentleman who was angry with his wife—and as a true disciple of various stress-relieving strategies, would dig a hole in the garden every night to relieve his anger. By the end of a couple of months, he had a hole big enough to make a swimming pool. He had a physique to be proud of–he was in superb physical fitness—but he was still an angry man! He worked out his anger, but when it kept returning, what he needed to do was confront his wife with what it was in her words/actions that was making him so angry. We will, in later chapters, go into details of how to deal with resentment and conflict.

Strategy to deal with an emotion:

1. Recognize it.
2. Own it: accept that you feel it.
3. Verbalize it: express it in words to yourself or to someone else.

4. Express it: take part in a physical activity to express your emotion. In short, act it out.
5. If a negative emotion persists or returns, reassess the situation. A confrontation may be necessary.

In all of this, a predominant feeling of "I" is happening. Here, 'I' denotes and encompasses "Self knowledge," or a very distinct understanding of the workings of one's innermost core. Self-knowledge does not come from birth. While there may be small inputs from a very young age, it is basically a process of practice – a practice of questioning yourself, time and again and coming up with answers. This process continues over a lifetime—in short, there is no end to this course of study.

Self-knowledge begins when you ask yourself, "Who am I?" You can answer this question by saying, "I am Sanjay Bansal." You may further add that you are a man or a woman, then go on to add physical traits like your height and weight, age, occupation and so on. But beneath all this, is the lingering question.

"Who am I really?" What are your most intimate secret thoughts, needs, values and feelings?

Who am I? Your Thoughts, Needs and Values

An emotionally healthy person functions in relation to three entities:

1. In relation to self.
2. In relation to others.
3. In relation to society.

Figuratively a person's thoughts take place in the outermost layer of his brain. One is always aware of them. If you have distorted, negative thoughts you will probably feel unhappy. Your thoughts shape your life. Hence, the power of "positive thinking."

Training your mind to think positively is a challenging discipline and requires continuous practice. Today, scientific research shows that positive thinking can also safeguard your physical health by protecting you from disease and helping you to heal from your disease.

With the help of this tool called '*positive thinking*' we can go ahead with the next step of identifying your needs.

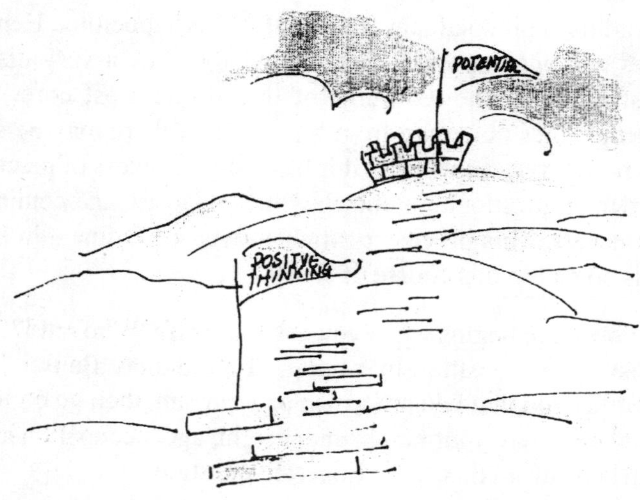

Abraham Maslow has postulated a theory of hierarchy of needs. According to him, people struggling with hunger can hardly be expected to think about higher needs like Love. Once the basic need for food is met, other needs arise. The most primitive needs are those related to *survival* – food, clothing and shelter. Next comes the need to feel *physically safe and secure*. Once this is also fulfilled, we come to a person's *emotional needs*. If these needs are met, a person gets in touch with his need for respect and esteem; and once this is met, comes the ultimate step – *self-actualization*, or the realization of one's full potential. Mind you, a very few people evolve that far. Hence, they are called visionaries: the Ramakrishna Paramahansas and Vivekanandas of this world fall into this category. We, mere mortals, will aspire for one step less, and in case destiny decries it so, it is possible that one of us, may be able to reach that final step. So we will go step by step, for they say.

"A journey of a thousand miles begins but with one step." Chinese proverb.

Physiological needs—like food, clothing and shelter.
Safety needs—like security, safety to your person and to your belongings.
Love needs—both love and esteem needs pertain to a person's emotional needs in relation to his ownself and to others.
Esteem needs.
Self-actualization needs.

Becoming aware of your needs is an important step in getting to know yourself. As you continue with practice, you will identify more and more needs, some specific ones, and you will seek ways to meet them. Through this process you will become aware of another component of yourself – *your values.*

Your values are your rules for behaviour, more simply what you view as right and wrong. The first few ones are learnt from your family, from your surroundings, and later on, you continue to work them out for yourself. Values assign positive or negative "weightage" to things and lead to decisions. Values are both conscious and unconscious. Sometimes, you can state them in words and sometimes, they remain as an 'I feel' entity and influence your behaviour without your awareness. People who are well acquainted with themselves, are keenly aware of their values, and can choose their behaviour without confusion. For example, cheating in examinations is never an option for a person with values. Sadly, in today's world, many malpractices and corrupt dealings are considered quite normal. Would any of us consider jumping a queue as a wrong or using a recommendation to bypass others as anything but one's right or bribing one's way out of a situation as not the accepted thing?

Trivial, you may say; or this is the way of the world. But what happens when the next, not so innocent or trivial set of wrongs comes to be gradually accepted as normal? Before we slip into that morass of contorted values, let us take a close look at values.

You can discover your values by answering these few questions:

1. Would I be willing to publicly acknowledge this value?
2. How faithfully will I stand by this value when it is challenged, or when the act it implies brings negative consequences?
3. Do I consistently and repeatedly act in line with these values?

One can draw the example of Mahatma Gandhi's life, and his involvement with our freedom struggle, armed with the weapons of *Ahimsa* and passive resistance. Neither the prospect of long terms of imprisonment, nor the pressures of many powerful people made him waver from the values that he chose to believe in. Neither was he

guaranteeing success. He went about adhering to his value system and his beliefs. People who are emotionally healthy are not only able to recognize their emotions; they feel free to express them and also to act upon them when required.

Today, one routinely hears statements like today's generation has no values and today's youngsters are very selfish and so on. This unfortunately seems to be true to a large extent with all sections of society and the youngsters would reply, "You were fortunate to have role models whom you could emulate. Today, who are our role models? Family and corrupt members of society who continuously din into us that it is okay to give or take a bribe, okay to cheat on your tax returns, okay to indulge in sharp practices as it is a very competitive world, crime ridden angst filled movies, music that glorifies a sex and drug culture, or sportsmen whom we worshipped only to find they have feet of clay?"

The ball is in the court of the elders to answer the frustrating questions of today. Who went wrong and where? They say that after a war, the loser country slogs it out to develop into a strong economy. Germany and Japan are instances of places where the devastations and hardships imposed by war have been nullified with some backbreaking effort on the part of the citizens of these countries. In the process, they have erased the horrible past where they were known as the traditional villains, and earned for themselves a reputation as hard working people. They have also found it in their hearts to be contrite about their past misdeeds. Did we get our freedom too easily? Have we been in too much of a hurry to see the good life that somewhere along the way, we forgot to be sensitive to human needs? Or did we neglect our newer generations in the pursuit of wealth and prosperity? Worse, did we teach them wrong values by either the sins of commission or omission?

I recollect a story I read sometime in my teens. A kind-hearted man was extremely perturbed to see the difficulties of the butterfly when it was trying to come out of its cocoon. He painstakingly split each cocoon that he collected with his fingernails so that the butterfly could come out without a struggle. In doing so, he never realized that the butterfly would never be able to fly again. Likewise, parents who have seen some tough times try to protect their wards from any difficulties they may have to face, thus denying them the discipline of struggle and self-establishment that worked so well in their own case.

It is not as if we as a race alone are in need of EQ. In fact, this is a universal phenomenon, though we may feel we need it more only because we know our own lifestyles; because we understand ourselves better than we understand others. Half the battle is won, for EQ is about primarily understanding self.

"Realize that you have sixteen waking hours, three or four of which should be devoted to making a silent conquest of your mental machinery. The failure to cultivate the power of peaceful concentration is the greatest single cause of emotional breakdown. A few hours of the sixteen will suffice; only let them be hours of daily dedication." These are the words of Sir William Osler, and if not hours, even a little lesser than an hour would be sufficient to go over the emotions experienced in that day.

•••

IV

Different Stages of Life

Men never knew what is right
So, caught between a promise and a doubt
They first made windows to let in light
And then made curtains to shut it out.

Our scriptures describe different stages of life as those of *balya, yauvana, grihasta, and vyragya*, or those of childhood, youth, family life and its commitments, and the last one of turning towards God. No book of science has done better than that! Various changes take place in a person's life, some with his knowledge and concurrence and some without it. When a person sees the pattern of his life, he can assume some control and make conscious choices that would not be possible otherwise. According to psychoanalyst Erik Erikson, there are eight stages of life, (four of these are devoted to *balya* or childhood, one to *yauvana*, two to the *grihasta ashrama* and the last to *vyragya*) each having its own significance, dilemmas and

contribution towards moulding the next stages—most often on a permanent basis, thereby leaving its indelible impression on life. Hence, the role of each and every stage in moulding life patterns is important, and our necessity is to study our life patterns carefully. Most often remedial action is possible; change can be brought about by us, and in a few cases with the help of specialists in that field.

Infancy, which is up to Age Two : This is an age where the infant receives affection from one and all. This love is unconditional as no adult expects any sort of reward from the infant. The infant also knows that his needs will be met; if he is hungry, he will be fed. If he is hurt due to some problem, he would be consoled. Often he is carried by some adult on his shoulder, patted on the back and cooled some soothing words. Most often, the infant sleeps, rocked to comfort. The infant is thriving on the love and affection he is getting as also on the surety of his needs being met. Occasionally, it happens that the infant can well be a neglected one. In extreme cases, children who suffer unwantedness, may get involved in criminal activities. In this case, most often the reasons for deviant behaviour are simple, very down to earth and quite common in today's world. It could just be that the infant has been left in the hands of a care-giver who is not paying sufficient attention to his needs. The infant might have been left to crying, or given a whack on his bottom. I have heard of stories of another nature where the care-giver laced the infant's milk with a shot of opium to make him sleep peacefully. It is a moot question whether the soothing sleep of opium or letting the child cry and feel neglected is better. A choice between the devil and the deep sea indeed!

If neglected or abused at this stage, and deprived of natural love and caring, the infant may well go through life mistrusting the world.

At this age, the qualities that get inculcated by default are love and care and trust. Obviously, the opposite is that of mistrust.

The Age of the Toddler: Age 1 to 2. Here you find that the little youngster, ever so cute, has a mind of his own! He knows how to demand things that are beyond his need, for example, his favourite toy—or to be carried by his parent not because he is hurt, but because he 'wants to'. Though dependent on his parents, he learns to be a separate person with self-will. He is learning the power of autonomy. What should be the parent's response to his autonomy, or his assertion of will? A difficult question indeed! Most often, in this phase, where the toddler is too young to understand, it is better to more or less give in. Psychologists opine that *if thwarted at this stage, the toddler learns to feel inadequate and ashamed. As an adult, this person may remain dependent and have feelings of inadequacy*. At this age, it is autonomy versus dependency and inadequacy.

Pre-school Stage: Age 3 to 5. This is a stage, and most parents will agree, when the child is extremely curious. 'Why', 'where', 'how' and 'when' are the barrage of questions that are aimed at parents all day through. The child is exploring the world surrounding him, and as yet, there are very few external influences, barring that of TV. The child moves to touch a precious object on the table that you have brought home from a foreign tour. He finds the beautiful crystal object fascinating! As he picks it up, you yell, "Don't touch it!" The object, precariously held in those little hands, drops and breaks. The child halts in his tracks with a bewildered expression, looks around, and begins to cry. If at that stage, he is further rebuked, and the incidence of the broken object becomes a family story of loss and negligence, the child is likely to grow up with a lack of initiative. This is an age when the child begins to use initiative. Accidents are prone to happen in this stage of exploration, and the question here is not to overlook or encourage such accidents, but to try to encourage the child's initiative without disastrous results. After all, in the above-mentioned instance, the breakage of the crystal object might have well resulted in the child sustaining a bleeding injury! Severe rebuke at that stage brings on a sense of shame at his own initiative. The answer may well be in keeping precious heirlooms or breakable objects away from the child's reach. And if an accident happens, console the child that it is sad that the object has broken, but that you are glad that he is not hurt and that he has learnt for himself that objects do break—and so it is better to keep away from them! It is the same in the case of fire and fireworks that so often attract a child's attention. On the other hand, if the same story is often the topic of conversation highlighting the carelessness of the child, it would reinforce the feeling of guilt. This is not to say that a single instance alters the potential of the child, but a recurring pattern would definitely do so. *This is* the *age of initiative versus guilt.*

School Age: Age 6 to 12. This is the age when a parent has definite expectations from the child, and also inculcates in him the quality of industriousness, of working to complete a task. On the basis of the learning of the three previous stages, plus the teaching of 'putting in effort' at this point in time, the child begins to thrive. He has the confidence to pursue his self-chosen goals at play and at school. He has his own reason for playing with this boy or not wanting to play with that boy. There will be minor skirmishes, but the child learns to tackle them by ignoring them, fighting back or even complaining to an adult. But the fact is, he has the initiative to make his own decisions. A healthy child works well and functions well in society. He has his goals in terms of lessons, his likings in terms of his friends or the games he wants to play, is aware of his limits when it comes to simple things like playtimes, permission to stay outdoors, and is aware of the expectations from him.

It is Important that the Expectations be Realistic: Failing to live up to the targets set by others in anticipation of performance can be a very trying experience for the child. Most often the targets set by parents are arbitrary and are a fulfilling of the universal desire that their offspring should be the best – in class, games or other curricular and co-curricular activities. While it is not a crime to hope for the same, it is wise to accept the existing limitations set by the actual performance of the child. Some improvement from the base line can be expected by industriousness, a quality to be ingrained at this age, but one should not expect miracles. Castigation for failure to perform to the exacting standards of the parents/society further undermines the confidence of the child, and the poor performance will continue. Further, the child may well be burdened by guilt – for not measuring up to his parents' expectations that could in turn lead to a loss of self-esteem, or at the other end of the scale lead to a stubborn mindset and antisocial feelings.

In this context, one has to face another prime motivator, for good or for bad: the TV. This item has intruded into our lives to such an extent that conversations in families have been reduced to monosyllables. Playtime, much beloved by children of yesteryears is non-existent, and sleeping habits and eating times are dictated by TV. Worse the quality and content of the programmes may well have a deleterious effect on the child's development. It has been time and again proved that this single item has influenced young minds in the wrong way. It is essential that the parent comes to a clear understanding with his child about the hours and programmes they would be allowed in this respect. A difficult situation for the parent indeed!

The sum total of autonomy, initiative and industriousness, all enveloped in love make for the child's personality. *If this development fails, the child in later years, as an adult, will lack confidence and perform poorly. He will be mistrustful of the world in general, lack initiative and* suffer *from a feeling of inadequacy and guilt.*

All the preceding stages fall under the head of *balya* in our heritage. You will notice that Dr. Ericson has placed great emphasis on the childhood phase. This is because nearly eight percent of the learning takes place during this phase. Be it a new language or values, this phase is the foundation on which the rest of that basic learning lies. Again, this or any other step should not be taken as a mere step towards the achievement of a larger goal. Every stage is lived through and accepted as a continuous phase of learning and not as, "If you want to gain something in later years, you must be willing to forego, work hard for, plan today to be able to achieve that at a later date." Every stage is fulfilling in itself, is entire in itself, and is not as mere preparation for the tomorrows to come. Yes every stage, every single day increases your learning of life, of understanding your inner self; the more you comprehend the truth of your values, the value of your emotions, suddenly you will find that life is richer. Now we go onwards to the next stage.

Adolescence: Age 13 to 20. For a youngster living in any country this is a particularly trying time. This is a time when many decisions have to be taken and the need for a course to be chartered out regarding a career or means of livelihood. This is also a phase when most youngsters are likely to be at loggerheads with their parents, teachers and generally every one of the older generation. Sometimes, there seems to be a conflict of interests, and it is not unusual to find many youngsters in a confused state of mind. They are in search of an identity. An identity created by their inner self, based on initiative, autonomy and industriousness nurtured in the previous years. If all is going well, he will further reinforce his identity in his social circle, as the leader or a follower.

An adolescent would have developed a strong sense of self, goals, and timing. He picks out role models to emulate and grows in confidence and self-definition. At a recent seminar on the reason for declining standards in medical education, the blame was placed squarely at the door of exactly this issue by stalwarts in the field of teaching who have invested a lifetime in nurturing young minds. Not only is there a lack of role models to emulate, there is a conflict of interest as well. Parents to whom the child has looked to for guidance apart from love and affection, seem not to be the people the children believed them to be. It is like they are seeing their parents in new colours, and the predominant ones unfortunately seem to be various shades of gray! Let us look at a simple queue at a railway reservation counter. The young thirteen year old sees that none respect the queue. His own father has used a short cut by having his mother stand in the ladies queue to buy tickets for the entire family for the simple reason that this one was shorter. In recent years, this queue has turned out to be one of the longest as everyone uses the same trick! A very small instance you say, and that you cannot believe that minor instances like this alter a person's value system, which in turn alters the equilibrium of his emotional quotient. Let us look at this from another angle. How many such small instances piled up one on top of another in the course of daily life would in your opinion be required to alter a person's values? Remember, the guidance is coming from a person the child trusts the most. It is a betrayal of sorts and leads to confusion about the rights and wrongs. On one side is the dilemma of, "My father cannot teach me something that is wrong," weighed against, "but he is doing the wrong thing!"

The same goes for smoking, driving rashly, or lying in the matters of taxes and ration cards and, of course, our quintessential scourge, giving and accepting bribes. It is possible that some of you may believe that I am talking of a Utopian society where all this is not possible. All this is okay in theory, but the practicalities of it are not really workable!

But who made the rules? Who let the world slip a couple of notches where a *wrong* committed by hundred people got the sanction of society and is labeled *right*?

We need to detach ourselves for a little while and reconsider matters. We are standing at the crossroads from where we have to take hard decisions. As long as we remain in a materialistic society there is no point in pontificating about what is wrong with our education system and so on. While much is wrong with the education system, more is wrong with the values we are inculcating in our children. We cannot teach them to keep the streets tidy while we throw our garbage indiscriminately. We cannot teach them that smoking is wrong while smoking ourselves. The mere cloak that "I do not smoke in front of my parents" is not enough, Good values mean that you do not do a thing you do not believe in, and whether in the open or behind closed doors is immaterial.

Hundreds of these signals reach our youth and children everyday. This hampers the development of the identity they wish to establish, and puts them in conflict with surroundings. They cannot feel secure in an ever-changing value system. Some equate security with the material comforts and bank balances. While I would not at all deny that it is comfortable to have money, accumulating wealth, cannot be the sole criterion of security. And in terms of security, bundles of cash, I am afraid, are a poor substitute for the wealth of values. I wish you to recall the heart-rending statements of a wealthy and very well placed parent after the arrest of her son for drunken driving in the recent past.

What has rearing a child have to do with Emotional Intelligence? Everything. For all emotions and their smooth flow, or they being tied into knots lies in childhood.

This is an age of identity versus confusion without a sense of timing and a sense of direction.

Young Adulthood: Age 21 to 40. One more step forward in the journey of life. At this stage, the young person wants to develop intimacy. The well-developed person wants to commit himself to work, to love and to a social group or community. He has finished his education or has taken the step towards that goal, and is poised to make that final commitment to his work, to his future career.

At about this time, for biological reasons apart from emotional ones, he wishes to develop an intimacy with the opposite sex. In a healthy, emotionally well-developed person, these decisions are taken without conflict with his innerself. It does not necessarily mean that he is not in conflict with his family. But he is at peace with his innerself regarding his decisions. As a full-fledged adult, he is within his rights to make his choices about his work and his life mate. Perceptions as to what the parents believe to be right regarding the choice of his work and his life mate could differ from those of his own. Each of them needs to stand by his values, even if they differ. A person with good EQ also understands the feelings of the other person, even when they differ from them.

We now get back to values, and the firm convictions of the inner self. Nowhere does it say that life will be like a fairy tale, "and they lived happily ever after." Sometimes choices can well mean deprivation and sacrifices. Sometimes they could result at your being alienated from your family. An emotionally well-developed individual would always make his decisions based upon the values of his innerself. These developments have to take place in the individual himself, and have nothing to do with the acceptance or the lack of it on the part of his family in any matter whatsoever.

The failure of this development leads to avoidance of intimacy, sexual promiscuity, isolation and destructiveness.

Adulthood: Age 41 to 60. In most societies it is called the prime of life. A time when a man makes his mark in his given field, makes money, and rears his family while thinking on a higher plane. Men in this age group govern society, in terms of money and ideology. To go back to Maslow's hierarchy of needs, once the basic needs of life and those of security are met, one can think of the higher needs, like esteem needs. He is at a stage of generativity. He moves through life taking pride in others' accomplishments, especially those of the children and young people. In the Indian context, he would have finished with the responsibilities bestowed upon him by tradition like the marriages of his children. The reason I state this is that in Western societies this responsibility is that of the young individual in the previous stage, and not that of the elder parent in this stage. This stage is that of the gr̥ihasta ashrama. A man burdened by conflict arising from his unmet emotional needs most often leans towards artificial pacifiers like a group of yes- men who bolster his ego irrespective of the rights and wrongs. He might be indifferent to, and authoritarian with his family and at his work place.

The failure of this stage of confidence and pride is that of self-involvement and failure to encourage others.

Older Adulthood: Age 61 onwards. To retain ego integrity is the goal of this stage. Having fulfiled his entire life's plans, the individual should be in a state of completeness, of fulfilment, of satisfaction. Nevertheless, he will find many things he could have done better in retrospective. But realizing that what has gone past is gone and retaining his ego integrity helps him to face death with serenity. A satisfaction of having done a certain thing in a certain way because of the convictions of that time—this is what ego integrity is all about. In a person with good value system, it is unlikely that his course of action or stand on matters would differ from time to time. Let this not be understood as obstinacy. A good ego integrity assures that a person will understand the changes and change himself as per the times, but his value system remains intact. On the other hand, a good value system accepts the changes. You can transpose this statement to various instances in the family or even business to find the truth in it.

Let alone personal life, accepting the changes has proved to be beneficial and the appropriate thing to do in century-old business houses too.

Started by the entrepreneurship of a single individual and nursed to reach commendable heights, the businesses continued to be family-held for another generation. They flourished—many a time with the succeeding generations trained in more than an adequate manner to take on the onerous responsibilities apart from having hands-on experience on the floor. Sometimes, looking at the rapidity of development, professional managers were employed with excellent results. These people have learnt to accept change and have in fact adapted to it as a motivating factor.

The adult who has not enjoyed the positive sides of each of these development stages experiences an increasing isolation and despair and fears death.

I do believe one ought to face facts. If you don't, they become the demons that haunt you. As long as one faces them, one is top dog. The important thing is not to steal oneself, but to face them calmly, easily – to get into the habit of facing them.

Dr. Hans Selye, whose concept of *'Stress'* is world-famous, declares: " If all efforts planned specifically to stimulate associative thoughts fail, there is no point in trying to force a solution by sheer stubbornness; it is best to let the problem slip from the sphere of conscious analysis and incubate in the unconscious. At this stage all we can do is to create conditions favourable to imaginative thinking. It seems that after we have saturated ourselves with all the material necessary for the appraisal of a new co-relation, we are invariably too close to this or that aspect to see it in true perspective. An unexpected solution to a problem is most unlikely to present itself when we are making desperate conscious effort to find it."

Each of the stages of life has a definite impact on a person's emotional intelligence. If childhood largely shapes individual EQ, the later years help him in turn to shape the EQ of people who come within his orbit. Improving upon EQ is a continuous affair which never ends, for a person who teaches actually learns more than the taught!

•••

V

Developing Self-esteem

We shall not cease from exploration, and the end of all our exploring will be to arrive where we started and know the place for the first time.

T.S. Eliot

One may wonder what self-esteem has got to do with EQ. I will say, "Everything!" It is only a person who understands himself as he is, and is in total satisfaction about who he is, who can try to understand others. If EQ is about understanding others and living your life in empathy to the feelings of others, then the most important step in that direction is to first understand yourself, and resolve conflict about your values and motivations.

At various times EQ has been easily defined as various things. Serious researchers in the field have not been able to exactly put their finger on it, and have time and again modified definitions. They range from street smartness to the voice of your conscience, to your sixth sense to the ability to express all your emotions completely. I am of firm belief that to understand one's emotional motivations, one needs to have good self-esteem.

How many people do you know who really believe in and respect themselves? People who are emotionally healthy, have high self-esteem; they know and like themselves. This does not imply that they think themselves to be perfect. On the contrary, such people accept that they have faults, and like themselves anyway—all the time trying to move away from their faults. They not only cherish their positive qualities, but also have learnt to accept the negative ones, even while they are trying to improve themselves. In contrast, a person who claims to be perfect has low self-esteem; that is why he denies his imperfections. 'So much attention to self is indulgent and selfish,' say the doubting Thomases, but the fact is that those who take care of themselves actually have more to offer to their families, friends and society.

Self-esteem is so crucial to emotional health that some psychologists use attitudes toward the self as criteria for evaluating mental health. The rationale is that poor self-esteem is closely linked to alcoholism, drug abuse, crime and violence, and the failure of children to learn. Poor self-esteem not only diminishes the individual, but also society.

One can enhance self-esteem in two ways.

One, by fostering a positive view of your inner self, and

Two, by developing a healthy relationship with your own outer self, your body.

How to View the Inner Self Positively

A simple way to do this is to practise making affirmative statements. These statements, called affirmations, can be once perceived as true now, or to be made true by means of practice. Affirmations empower people – that is, they make you feel effective. Affirmative ideas replace defeating messages.

To practise making affirmations, one must repeat positive messages so often that they embed themselves in the subconscious mind and manifest themselves in daily life. Affirmations are "I" statements, phrased positively, as in:

I can relax under stress.

I can be alone without being lonely.

I accept myself as I am.

Add statements of this nature, which are to your conviction, to this list.

Another helpful tool is to visualize yourself succeeding at a task or developing a quality that you desire. Visualizing success helps in building self-esteem, improving school performance and overcoming emotional problems. This keen desire helps you to work towards your visualized targets. It necessarily means that besides thinking positively, one must take actions. A simple flow chart would run like this:

- Note down your affirmations.
- Pursue activities — both occupational and recreational – that reflect your skills and interests.
- Be grateful. Appreciate what you have.
- Read good books and see good movies that let uplifting thoughts enter your mind – remember, you reap as you sow! Or as in computer language, GIGO – garbage in, garbage out.
- Surround yourself with friends who believe in you.
- Relax and have fun.
- Celebrate your success.

- Give and receive affection.
- Another suggestion for making desired affirmations become reality is, "acting as if" you have the quality you are seeking. This is called, "fake it till you have it!"

This is a useful tool not only for personal development but also in telling the sales persons how to make a successful sale. To illustrate with an example, acting cheerfully when you are not really feeling on top of the world, will help in getting adjusted to the situation, and a more congenial mindset will follow. You can say this is a positive effort on the part of the individual towards betterment. A similar example of visualizing is used in obesity clinics and self-help techniques to control weight. A photograph of a favourite film star or athlete is to be pinned up at strategic points like the refrigerator to act as a deterrent against overeating. In a reverse way, most salesmen capitalize on a person's dissatisfaction with himself and make the person believe that his situation is not acceptable. A certain company makes people believe that their homes are so ill kept that they cannot possibly make their surroundings healthy without using their product! A person with low self-esteem is rather defenceless against such tricks. The higher the self-esteem, the easier it is to see through these tricks.

Part of self-esteem is to like yourself for what you are, and not for what you do. Society's focus on achievement can result in overvaluing externals like how much money you make, the car you drive, or the position you hold. This subtly erodes self-esteem and creates a frenzy of striving to achieve according to society's standards. The problem is, when they fail, they think this reflects on their inherent capacities; when they make mistakes, these become their personal agonies.

The mistake is what a person does, not what a person is. Knowing that you are unique and worthwhile apart from your achievements and accomplishments and in spite of your failures and mistakes supports your self-esteem. When you confidently develop your image you will be less influenced by others and will not feel the necessity to bend yourself into knots to fit into other people's moulds.

To totally understand ourselves and our motivations when dealing with others, we need to use a yardstick to evaluate our own behaviour pattern. Many a time we are caught in a situation that could do with some analysis. It is not possible time and again to run to others for direction—so we will adapt a simple method wherein it is possible to conduct this analysis. The theory of Transactional Analysis deals with this in a simple way. It categorizes all actions on a simple basis that each human being has many personalities within himself. Every person has in himself numerous components that develop during early years called the Child, the Parent, and the Adult.

The child is characterized by spontaneity and curiosity. The child in you experiences many of your feelings. That is why you may feel like a child when you are angry or sad.

The parent is a collection of all the people who wielded authority over you in the past, like biological parents, other relatives and teachers. This conglomerate figure expresses your values.

The adult is the reasoning person who collects information, weighs facts and makes a rational meaning of them.

(These three types, child, parent and adult, are purely symbolic of the types they represent, and are not to be confused with or transposed with the real person in that relationship. In the succeeding paragraphs, when we discuss parent or child, we are not discussing a parent-child relationship. In fact, these three types can well be called by any other names like XYZ or John, Mary and George, except that when they are called Parent or Adult, their characteristics are easy to understand.)

Traits of Parent, Adult and Child

Parent	*Adult*	*Child*
Nurturing	Information giving	Loving
Tender	Fact finding	Impulsive
Helpful	Reality testing	Curious

Judegment making	Intelligent	Playful
Value conveying	Objective	Exuberant
Traditional messaging	Able to estimate probabilities	Spontaneous
Critical	Able to compute	Irresponsible
Selfish	Dispassionately	Manipulative

Every individual carries within himself some of the traits of each of these types – the whole personality depends on the preponderance as to which of these components is over-shadowing the others at that given point of time, or in reacting to a certain conclusion.

Let us consider the parent figure first. Parents can be of two kinds:

–Critical
–Nurturing

The **critical parent** reacts to the child in a predominantly negative and judgmental way. A person raised in this way can develop a negative self-concept that interferes with his emotional growth. A person who has heard condemning messages all through childhood, like no-good, lazy, fit for nothing usually adopts a "critical parent" as a permanent part of his personality and will continue to hear negative judgements from within even in his adult life.

In contrast, the **nurturing parent** reacts to a child positively as being cute, funny, industrious, achieving and so on. This child, on growing up to be an adult, carries a more self-approving "Parent" inside, and the accepting/nurturing messages heard in childhood are repeated throughout the adult life. These statements are confirming and support emotional health.

Part of being emotionally healthy is learning to adopt a nurturing parental attitude towards yourself. Those who received criticism and negative messages during childhood must work hard to change the negative internal messages into positive ones, so as to enhance self-esteem and enable emotional growth.

Examining the personalities within requires you to examine your childhood experiences and how they affect you. This can help you grow towards emotional maturity.

Examples of T.A. personalities:

1. On seeing an older child playing with a baby on a swing.
Parent: This better stop before someone gets hurt.
Adult: The baby seems to be enjoying this game, and the swing is protected on all sides.
Child: This is fun. I want to do it too.

2. On waking up in the morning still feeling sleepy.
Parent: Stay in bed, you need the rest.
Adult: If I stay in bed, I catch up on the rest, but I miss something else.
Child: (Fast asleep)

3. On seeing some pretty crystal objects in a shop.
Parent: Don't touch.
Adult: I wonder how much effort and craftsmanship goes into the making of each piece.
Child: They are so pretty. I want them all.

The theory of T.A. holds that everyone's personality includes the Child, Adult and Parent components. Being a nurturing parent to one's internal child and using ones internal adult to make realistic judgments fosters emotional health. And there will be times when the internal child completely takes over – and you must let this happen, as in the case of wrenching emotions.

The mention of T.A. here is to help you to delve into your personality using these tools. This can take you a long way in improving your self-esteem, and thereby your emotional health. To cultivate emotional health means to keep on growing, to continue to deal with the psychological changes life brings. Many of these changes are predictable and they help in knowing what lies ahead.

We've said that emotionally healthy people function in three different spheres – in relation to self, to others, and to society. So far we have been looking into the most important relationship in any one's life, the relationship to self, and to this end, we have looked into developing self-esteem by analyzing your actions with the help of simple tools. Now, let us look into the relationship with others.

Relationships with Others

As individuals, we need relationships with other people; it is normal and healthy to turn to relationships to meet some of our needs. However, a vast difference exists between meeting normal needs in relationships and becoming too dependent. An emotionally healthy person develops a balanced give-and-take attitude towards others.

Relationships are varied. These are the ones you have with your parents, which are different from the ones you have with your siblings or your friends. Friendships can vary tremendously. Your intimate love life is different from other relationships. All these form an interlinked connection that defines who you are.

Ideally people should develop a strong support system. This may consist of family, neighbours, friends at work, a mentor or advisor or even a self help group. In a relationship, the other person is ready to give, as well as to receive; so there should not be any embarrassment about asking support. Many are, however scared to open up and talk or to ask for support, as they are scared of "rejection."

Reaching out to other people usually does not lead to rejection, but in the beginning, one has to be willing to accept rejection and to handle it. If it doesn't work, one should be able to say, "I tried. It does not reflect on me. The other person has more needs." (Not the usual, he or she is very selfish/arrogant/thinks too much of himself and so on.) More often, when you reach out, you find that the other person is more than willing to be approached. So do not hesitate to form a relationship with others. At worst, you will have made an attempt; at best you would have made the first step towards a rewarding relationship.

Everyone knows this, but is afraid to act upon it, because they don't know how. Psychologists recommend the acronym, SOFTEN

- S—Smile
- O—Open posture
- F—Forward lean
- T—Touch
- E—Eye contact
- N—Nod.

You will find that it really softens the other person to offer you a helping hand in forming a relationship.

In the list of the characteristics of emotionally healthy people given below, you will notice that self-esteem is way up. Characteristics of emotionally healthy people are:

Have self-esteem.
Are confident that their behaviour is normal.
Are honest.
Accept themselves.
Don't take themselves too seriously.

Recognize that other people can enhance their lives but are not the sole source of their happiness.

Do not try to control things they cannot control.

Do not always seek approval from others.

Do not manipulate others to get their way.

Take responsibility appropriately but do not take too much responsibility for others.

Consider consequences before acting.

Deal with emotional pain by feeling and expressing it appropriately.

Be able to grieve when suffer losses.

Live with balance, not extremes.

Creatively express themselves, if inclined, by painting, writing, singing and other artistic activities.

Continue to mature mentally, emotionally and spiritually throughout their lives.

Refuse to tolerate inappropriate behaviour.

Disclose family problems when appropriate.

Validate and acknowledge their observations, feelings and reactions.

Now that we have gone into some of the basics of developing a strong emotional self, it is time to do a small test to see how one fares.

•••

VI

Your First Test

It is appalling that our technology exceeds our humanity.

Albert Einstein

To measure IQ there are specific tests that can be graded and exact marks given. These tests are so fine-tuned that there are organizations like the MENSA that can rate you; a certificate from this institute is a real feather in the cap. One cannot look for such a test and such an exact rating in the field of EQ. Neither are the tests specific in any way, nor the grading exact. Since one is dealing with a quality that in itself cannot be quantified, it is but natural that any test in this field will follow the same rationale.

Having said this, I must however emphasize that the tests do help in giving the person a basic idea of what the expected reactions of a person ought to be in a given situation, and how far out one is from the expected. The most important character in doing this test is being truthful about your own reactions. Most often one tends to second-guess the best possible answer, that is, pick the answer that one ought to pick, rather than the one that is your instinctive reaction. We do it all the time with the quiz we set out to answer from the Reader's Digest.

So before we start on the test which is quite simple, please affirm to yourself that you will mark the answers that are your true reactions to the questions, and not the ideal ones. This is not an examination that can shape the course of your career; treat it as a fun questionnaire from which you can pick up some insights about your own behaviour patterns. Remember, life is a never-ending test of sorts, and there are ever so many opportunities to learn and put to use in daily situations.

There are four options to each question and you may pick one of them as your option.

1. You are a student. You are hoping to get very good marks in Physics in your final examination. However, in your mid-term test, your score is only sixty percent. Will you:

a. Plan out a timetable by which you can do a more comprehensive study.
b. Resolve to work toward your goal by seeking the help of teachers/others who are qualified to teach.
c. Tell yourself that this is a lost cause and concentrate on other subjects where you have got a higher mark.
d. Try to talk your teacher into giving you some extra marks by telling her sob stories or telling her about the tremendous influence your father wields in society.

2. You are seated in an aeroplane. Suddenly, there is turbulence in the air and the ride becomes very bumpy. The captain switches on the fasten seat belts sign. Do you:

a. Continue to read your book or watch the movie.

b. Mentally go through all the 'in the event of an emergency' routine that was explained just before take off.

c. A little of both, 'a' and 'b.'

d. Do not like to give attention to such matters.

3. You have taken a group of seven-year old children along with your niece to a nearby park. These children live in the same or nearby building.. Suddenly, one of them starts crying because the others are not letting her play with them. Do you:

a. Not interfere in the matter and let the children resolve the issue among themselves.

b. Talk to her and help in finding out ways to make other kids play with her.

c. Tell her in a kind voice not to cry.

d. Distract her attention by telling her some story or amusing incident.

4. You are a door-to-door salesman dealing with consumer products. You have made more than a dozen calls, only to have doors shut on you every time. You are very discouraged.

a. Do you decide to call it a day and try again tomorrow?

b. Sit down and examine if your method of approach needs to be changed.

c. Try something new at the next call and keep on trying without stopping.

d. Decide that this line of work is not for you and resolve to make a change at the earliest opportunity.

5. You are the manager of an MNC that has a cross-section of people from different states, and some foreigners apart from a large number of locals. Someone makes a joke, a nasty one, about a certain state/community that you overhear. You know that this has been happening every now and then. Do you:

a. Ignore it. After all, it is just a joke.

b. Call the person to your office for a reprimand/talking.

c. Speak up then and there, in the presence of others, that such sort of an attitude will not do in your organization.

d. Suggest that the person better do an orientation course to help him adjust in a multi-lingual atmosphere.

6. Both you and your friend are driving to work. A rash driver nearly hits your car, but fortunately, there is no injury to yourselves or damage to the car. However, your friend is very angry and upset. You try to:

a. Say, "It's okay. No one is hurt."

b. Put on some good music and try to divert his attention.

c. In a show of comradeship, join him in heaping the choicest words of abuse at the errant driver.

d. Narrate to your friend how you have had similar near-mishaps in the past and this was not going to be the last time. One learns to live with such situations.

7. You and your spouse have suddenly got into one of those arguments that is threatening to go out of control. Both of you have resorted to personal attacks and have begun to call each other names. Do you:

a. Take a small break of 20 minutes and then continue the discussion.

b. Stop arguing and be silent, no matter what the other person says.

c. Say, you are sorry and stop. But insist that the other person says sorry too.

d. Stop for a minute, collect your thoughts, and say them as logically and calmly as you can.

8. You are the head of a team that has just been assigned a project. This project has run into problems and your first duty is to come up with a creative solution to this hurdle. Do you.

a. Draw up an agenda and allot time for each component of the programme so that everyone and every issue gets time and you have attended to all aspects.

b. Use the time to let the people in the team get to know one another so that they can work better.

c. Begin by asking each person how to solve the problem while the ideas are still fresh in their minds.

d. Start with a brainstorming session encouraging everyone to say what comes to their mind, no matter how wild.

9. Your three-year old is extremely timid and rather scared than shy about meeting new people and going to new places. Do you:

a. Accept that he is of a shy temperament and try to find out ways to shelter him from such experiences.

b. Take him to a child psychiatrist for help.

c. Purposely expose him to a lot of new people and situations saying that it is the only way for him to get over his fear.

d. Prepare a list of activities that challenge him without overwhelming him so that he can get used to the idea and slowly get over his fear.

10. You had learnt to play the sitar in your childhood. Before you could really master the art, you had to give it up for certain reasons. It has always remained a cherished dream that you should learn to play the instrument again. Now, you have a chance to learn. You have engaged a teacher to come everyday. Do you:

a. Hold yourself to a strict practice time everyday.
b. Pick music pieces that are slightly beyond your capability so that it offers a challenge.
c. Play only when you are in the mood to do so.
d. Ask for assignments that are way beyond your capabilities as a challenge that diligent practice can help you master these compositions.

That was the test! I am sure you have found it rather easy to do. And you are wondering why the questionnaire has so many day-to-day examples instead of tough management principles!

Simple. Because EQ is about daily life in all its aspects. Its applicability to management issues is to help us understand your motivations in dealing with your own emotions and those of other people in normal and abnormal situations.

The basics of emotional intelligence include:

- Knowing your feelings and using them to make life decisions that you can live with.
- Being able to manage your emotional life without being literally hijacked by it. That is, not giving in to depression, worry, anger and emotional outbursts.
- Persisting in your efforts and channeling your energies to the achievement of your goals.
- Empathy. Reading other people's feelings without them having to tell you how they are feeling.
- Handling feelings with skill and harmony; for example, being able to articulate the unsaid feelings of your group/family.

Your Answers and The Marks They Fetch You!

1. The capacity to work towards your goal in spite of trials and tribulations is a quality of good emotional intelligence. Answers 'A' and 'B' carry 20 marks each, while C and D get a zero.

2. Anything but 'D'. A, B and C carry 20 points each, but 'D' gets a zero as it shows a total lack of awareness of following your natural instincts under stress.

3. Emotionally healthy adults use opportunities like this to communicate with children and to get them to talk about their prejudices, fears, likes and dislikes. Answer 'B' fetches you 20 points while the other answers get a zero.

4. Optimism is a hallmark of the emotionally stable person. They use disappointments as challenges to get better and devise new methods and ideas to do better. They will not blame others, situations and indulge in self-pity. The marks go to 'C' – 20 marks while all the others will get nothing.
5. Instead of trying to change people and their prejudices, try to stop them from acting on them. It is advisable to be open and clear about the company's policy in front of everyone in a firm but gentle tone (no shouting and pulling rank to show them who's the boss) so that the message goes across to one and all. 'C' gets 20, while the others do not get any.
6. Getting the better of rage shows you the effectiveness in distracting the person from the focus of his rage, empathizing with him, and showing in perspective a less harmful way of expressing his feelings. While 'A' gets a zero, 'B' and 'C'get 5 each, and 'D'gets 20.
7. Take a break of 20 minutes or more. It takes at least that much time for all the hormones and impulses generated by rage to get negated. At the end of this period, you can see things in the right perspective and state your side clearly and calmly. 'A" gets a twenty, while the others do not fetch you any.
8. Creative groups work the best when comfort levels are at the highest. That is when all of them understand one another and feel free to express their thoughts without hesitation. So, it is 'B' that gets twenty, while the others, I am afraid do not get anything.
9. Children born with timid temperaments do well under parental guidance and push. However, this should not be to the point of scaring the child, ridiculing him or alienating the child, but with a series of gentle to more progressive plans to overcome the fear. While 'B' gets a five, it is 'D' that walks away with the twenty.
10. By giving yourself a moderate challenge, you are most likely to get into the flow of things. This way it will be a pleasurable activity rather than a stress-filled challenge. 'B" gets the assigned twenty marks, while the other answers do not score.

The highest score is 200. A nigh on impossible score for a mere mortal. An average score would be 100. Generally, one would expect to score a little over a hundred. The higher you go, the better for you, unless of course, you are imagining a 'you' that really does not exist. Less than 100 would probably mean that you have very rigid views and it is better that you think over things a bit and attempt again! Generally, a score of about 130 shows you to be a well-balanced individual.

> "*My creed is this:*
> *Happiness is the only good.*
> *The place to be happy is here.*
> *The time to be happy is now.*
> *The way to be happy is to make others so.*"
>
> *Robert G. Ingersoll, Motto.*

●●●

Part 2

Introduction to Emotions

Mankind spent the better part of the last century smothering away a person's natural feelings. Prior to these times, man reacted spontaneously to the situations. Then came the value-system of the society that said: No. Emotions are like unbridled horses that need to be controlled. And society set about to lay rules that governed the living patterns of people – from a young child to the behaviour at a funeral. Society laid emphasis on intellectual development

to such an extent that it became the Frankenstein monster that threatened to over-rule man, its creator. As time passed the intellect of man reached its pinnacle. Man proved to his own kind that the pursuit of knowledge was paying off in a big way. By conquering space, inventing treatments to hitherto unknown diseases and charting a lifestyle of sheer luxury, thanks to his myriad inventions man set about his new goals. Then along the way he realised to his chagrin that he was becoming a robot, a automaton who could create a supercomputer with his brain but unfortunately had just about the same amount of emotion in him. It was as if his very intellect was killing him; his pursuit of knowledge to the exclusion of all else was being counterproductive and human values fell to the dust somewhere along the way.

Fortunately, he did an about-turn and decided to take stock of things before becoming a nerd. He realized that with all his intellect, man is not a solitary animal, and certain skills are required to live in harmony with his family, and with society. To do so, he first had to learn to live with himself; to be aware of all his emotions that he suppressed in the quest for intellectual prowess.

He delved into his psyche and came up with solutions that were actually man's natural instincts of a century back. He now faced a strange situation of unlearning all the teaching in this area before he began to orient himself to the "new" concept of Emotional Intelligence. In this quest, we go about dissecting minutely each of man's predominant emotions, in a bid to unlearn the past and put in fresh inputs.

•••

VII

The Nurturing Emotion—Affection/Love

Put away the book, the description, the tradition, the authority, and take the journey of self-discovery: Love! And don't be caught in opinions and ideas about what love is or should be. When you love, everything will come right. Love has its own action. Love, and you will know the blessings of it. Keep away from the authority who tells you what love is and what it is not. No authority knows and he who knows cannot tell. Love, and there is understanding.

J. Krishnamurti

The first of these is Love. Our current learning has shackled us down so much that we are reticent about calling this emotion by its original name. That being as it may we cannot deny the existence of this emotion or its other forms, like, affection and care. Respect and a near celestial love are the further offshoots of this emotion.

There are ever so many poetic and literary definitions of love with which we can fill pages; we are all aware and conscious of this abstract feeling in our lives in relation to someone or the other, but what we are looking for here is how this feeling, this emotion can help us to better our own selves in the first instance, and then help us in our relationship with others around us. For in acquiring the capacity to use our emotions fully, we do need to look at this poetic emotion, love in a more prosaic way – in its day-to-day applications in our daily lives.

We will start with the contention that love is the most nurturing emotion mankind has.

The parents love their two-year old no matter what. They love him if he troubles them. They love him even if he keeps them awake the whole night, every night. They love him even when they've to take the trouble to rush to the hospital. They love him even when he throws up on mother's new sari. The child too recognizes his parents and smiles, laughs and coos at them whenever he sees them. He is happy to be with them—so much so that all his problems in his little world seem to vanish once he is in their arms. This is called unconditional love. Love that is there, no matter what. Love that expects no returns.

Sadly, as the years pass, this very love becomes conditional. The same doting two-year old is now a five-year old. Slowly, his parents expect him to study well and behave well. Nothing wrong in that as such. But sometimes, statements such as, "Mummy will cook your favourite dish if you say all the nursery rhymes nicely. If not, your brother will get his choice," or "Daddy loves you because you come first in class." This signals a reciprocal action on part of the child to be his parent's favoured one, or in short, to be the recipient of their love. It then becomes conditional love. You do this for me and then you will be loved by me, is the underlying implication of all these statements. A lovely emotion has been reduced to a quid-pro-quo state.

While this is not a threat to extract better performance/behaviour from the child, (or the adolescent or as he grows to be a young adult with the passing years) it does send signals that a certain type of behaviour elicits a certain amount of emotion. Manipulation by both parties begins. The child understands it as, if I perform well, my parents will like me, or do such and such a thing for me; so he tries to comply with their demands. The child also understands that he has to hide his own feelings and vulnerabilities because these qualities are not acceptable to his parents or society. So the child actually puts on a performance by denying these unapproved actions to get the maximum benefit out of his parents or teachers.

Unfortunately, sometimes, in spite of his best efforts, he may not be able to do so. Let us suppose his parents would like him to be a topper in class, (which parent does not wish this for his child?) but the child in spite of his best efforts fails to make the grade. He is then castigated by the parent and goaded to perform better. There is a strong possibility that the child will rebel by discovering various tactics to evade extra classes, or changing the marks on the report card. In one instance, to escape punishment a child told the teacher that his grandparent had passed away, when he was very much alive!

The parent's actions have been motivated by love. But the parent has acted emotionally, rather than with his emotions. There is a world of difference in acting emotionally and in acting with emotional intelligence! In an emotionally intelligent statement, the parent would assure his offspring that he is loved no matter what, and that the love he gets from his family is not proportional to his performance, but is constant. Statements that say, "we love you and we will work together to overcome your problems", will further augment it.

This is not a book on Parenting—nevertheless, the seeds of emotional relationships are sowed in childhood, hence it is imperative to keep going back to those tender years to see the effect of adult statements and behaviour on children. It is to help the parent sow the seeds of a good emotional state in his child, even if he himself was deprived of it. If he gets over his problems by accepting them, he can help his child.

It is a fact that a child, who is burdened by guilt, or by a reciprocal quid-pro-quo arrangement of love, will continue to behave in the very same fashion as an adult. In all his relationships, he encounters a carrot being dangled in front of him - "If you do this for me, I will like you better," or " I will give you a good confidential report if you tow the line I laid out." How many times as adults have we seen this statement made to us? Perhaps the seeds of this behaviour go back to conditional love received by the person in his childhood. These are the result of strokes he received as a child that said.

How can we love you if you do this, or not do this?

If you don't act the way I think you should act, then I will reject you.

You are totally unacceptable to me if you do not behave in such and such manner; if you do not love my family, do not agree to everything. I say I will not accept you.

If you do as I say, I will love you.

I give so much of my time and money to you; you must do what I say.

These are some examples of adult transactions that are the outcome of this conditional love.

This conditional love has created many knots of psychological trauma in our lives, and we now need to work at untying them.

So we will now modify the definition of love as.

"Actively caring and accepting the others as they are."

Translated into human relationships, we get a perspective of love easily enough. Parents and children love each other, brothers and sisters love each other, friends love each other, husband and wife love each other and so on. We have also seen how the wrong signals in childhood are likely to influence an adult's behaviour pattern *vis-à-vis* love.

In the larger context of working relationships and attitude to society, one can say love is understood to be liking, caring and many times even duty.

We in India are very duty-conscious. It has been ingrained in us by centuries of teaching that duty is everything. Sometimes, we reduce every relationship to duty, which reduces us to mere automatons. It is our duty to look after our children, it is our duty to respect our teachers, it is our duty to obey our superiors at work, and it is our duty to look after our elderly parents. If we substitute the word 'love'– in thought and deed for the word 'duty' – the world would be full of caring rather than the imperatives, which seem so forcefully thrust on us. It is not too late to start, as being emotionally intelligent is a continuous process, and arduous effort on our part can alter our ingrained thinking.

In Management

Where does love figure in the work arena, you may ask. How can love be a ruling factor in the management zone? In the *Natya Shastra* of *Bharata*, the word *Sringara* that depicts love is further subdivided into various types of love that include *sambhoga* or the sexual type, and *vatsalya* or affection and *bhakti* or worship. In normal parlance, we have substituted the words 'caring' and 'liking' for love. Once you accept "caring" as a work place principle, it is not difficult to visualize the role of love in that area.

Are we not supposed to love/like the work we are doing?

Should we not like to work in that particular setup?

Should we not like our colleagues and superiors in the work place?

Should we not like the underlings who clean up the place everyday?

Are we not supposed to care/like the clients we serve day in and day out?

'Love' and 'like' here are not fawning words, words that mean, "I look after your needs as long as you look after me." 'Love' and 'like' are words that make the workplace a place you love to go, the people you work with are people whom you love to meet, and the job you are doing is not a compulsion, but something you enjoy doing. There might be some situations where you are tempted to say, "why should this happen to me, I hate everyone and everything here; in fact, I hate this job." A mindset that will make you think in terms of, "as long as I am here, let me do this job well and like my surroundings; I can keep a lookout for something else," is a perfectly sensible one. This sort of a mindset can only happen if you are willing to begin to like the present situation. You can make a beginning by liking one person, or one aspect of your job, rather than hope to instantly go by the principle of universal love.

Mr. Raman has been observing Sethi for some time now. Normally a good worker who meets his deadlines, Sethi seems to be off-colour lately and his performance has dropped a few notches. He also appears to be a trifle moody. Mr. Raman should

1. Ignore him saying it is not his problem. If he does not pull his weight, the administration will give him his just dues.
2. Call him to his office and give him some tough talk about his performance not being up to the mark.
3 Call him to his office and gently probe to see if there are some reasons that are the cause for his poor performance.

Most often, 1 and 2 are the patterns followed. But an emotionally intelligent manager will opt for No. 3. For him to be emotionally intelligent, he should have been a child brought up with plenty of love from childhood that comes naturally to him, or he should be a person who understands that his own childhood has been somewhat lacking and goes about remedying that shortfall. When Mr. Raman used tactic 3, he was able to elicit from Sethi that his marriage was going through some problems and he was consequently very troubled about it. Now we come to the next issue.

1. That is his personal problem and has nothing to do with his work. The office cannot suffer because of his personal reasons.
2. Ask him to take leave of absence to sort out his problems while the office allocates that work to someone else.
3. Talk to him to see if you can help in any way; suggest a counsellor. Help him by showing concern for him and reassuring him that you are there for any help that he may require. Just listening to his problem would lighten his burden.

Again, 1 and 2 are, the archetypal answers, but 3 is the emotionally intelligent answer. While this does not make excuses or exempt Sethi from doing his job, it does help him to cope with his problems. While taking leave may be the easy way out for the organization, some extra work will probably help to keep his mind occupied, once he is aware that he is not harbouring a secret, but sharing his problem with his colleagues.

The other questions are:

1. Is this uncalled for interference in his personal life?
2. Who has the time and patience to go into such problems of the workforce? Everyone has problems and this is not the place to play doctor to him.
3. Is this a good example of caring and a nurturing relationship between various members of the workforce?

You will notice that at no point was there interference in Sethi's personal life. Like a good counsellor, Mr. Raman was willing to listen when Sethi wanted to talk. And yes, he did find time to listen to Sethi. One can say that Mr. Raman, with his caring attitude, helped Sethi to cope with his problem. It is not even necessary or obligatory for Sethi to give him a blow-by-blow account of the daily happenings in his house. Neither did Mr. Raman probe. At the end of the day, Mr. Raman would have the satisfaction of caring for one of his broods, and Sethi would have the consolation that someone cared enough for him to ask, and to be there for him when he wanted to ventilate his innermost feelings. It is likely that the concern Sethi was shown in this instance, would make him do the same for another person at another time. It is such instances of caring that translate to love or vatsalya in the workplace.

Love–The Actual Feeling of It

There are some of us who cannot feel the feeling of love for others. It was trained "out" of us by the traumas of childhood. Men (often unknowingly) tend to suffer more from this disability than women, and tend to avoid close relationships and even in a close relationship, hesitate to articulate the words—I love you.

If this is a problem you think you have, the most important step you can take is to decide you want to feel love, and whether you want to receive love. Let us look at these three simple words: I LOVE YOU. The ability to say these words with feeling is essential. The ability to appropriately express these words in a non-sexual context to men, women and children is a good indicator of emotional health. As a race, we are extremely embarrassed by such outpourings of affection. We even tend to dismiss this off with, "you know I love you, so what is this about saying it." I have mentioned that there need not be a sexual connotation to the word 'love'. For the sake of Indian sensibilities, I will substitute it with "like." Time and again, psychologists have proved that.

The more of love/liking you pour into a person, you enable that person, in turn, to give away to others that much of this positive emotion.

You are enhancing his self-esteem by unconditionally loving (liking) him.

Increased self-esteem leads to an emotionally healthy person.

Love—the Physical Expression

Soft toys, particularly teddy bears are an epitome of love. One loves to hug them. Hugging is a natural expression of love between any two people of any gender in some parts of the world. We are particularly inhibited in this manner and literally shy off such physical contact. Perhaps if we get over the hang-up of sexual connotations of such physical contact, we will be able to indulge in hugging at least a person of the same gender as we would be a child. Basically, it is treated as an expression of love. We find that surrogate methods of gifting teddy bears for Valentine's day and Friendship day and even 'as a get-well soon' message has come to stay in our country. May be, just may be, we are opening our doors to receive some affection, and when we receive some, we will be able to give more!

The continuous practice of Emotional Intelligence helps to open our minds to the better exchange of love—and thus enhancing our EQ with every single transaction.

●●●

VIII

Freedom from Fear

The only thing we have to fear is fear itself.

Franklin D. Roosevelt

Separated from his parents for the first time and sent into a new environment, a child feels fear. He cries.

The young child fears the repercussions from the teacher when he does not do his homework. He finds ways to distract attention from himself by playing the sympathy card in the form of a stomach

ache or fever. Any logical or illogical reason will do to get him out of the situation.

Growing older, he fears examinations; perhaps as a sign of evaluation of his performance, which could have telling effects on his future.

Faced with an animal, many of us fear for the potential injury it may cause to our self. Why there are some who fear a creature as small as a rat? Perhaps due to an inherent dislike for it.

Face to face with a robber or criminal, we fear for our possessions as well as our being. We run for safety, while at the other end of the spectrum, someone may faint with fear.

When the doctor diagnoses an alarming disease in case of any of our loved ones, we fear the consequences of the disease.

The management trainee fears deadlines he cannot meet.
The businessmen fear financial ups and downs.
The farmer fears the vagaries of the weather.
When our country is at war, we fear for our country.
We fear cyclones, floods and earthquakes.
A horror movie is enough to scare the best of us.

This list can go on *ad infinitum*, as each of us have our own fears.

Fear is a realistic response to a perceived danger in the environment. Fear is normal, fear is natural and fear is helpful. Fear is a physiological response, just like we need to eat when we feel hungry, or drink water when we feel thirsty, we fear a thing that we perceive to be causing us harm. Fear generates the famous fight or flight response in our bodies that give us the strength to tackle that fear. It could be in one of many ways. In each of these examples, one can notice that the reaction to the action can be by flight, aggression, avoidance or other devious methods like blaming others or even more negative traits like lying, cheating and so on.

This is where we step in to analyze the effects of fear. The first step is to try to understand whenever possible the reason for the fear. Then a positive step can be taken to overcome the initial source from which the fear has generated. It is quite obvious that all sources of fear cannot be tackled by the individual, as in the case of war, riots, accidents, floods and so on. Thus the famous saying.

"What cannot be cured must be endured," comes into play.

By such an analysis, we will be able to control our emotion—the emotion of fear so that it does not go haywire. Psychologists will tell you that fear gone haywire is the root cause of most of the phobias they treat in a day-to-day basis apart from anxiety disorders and depression.

Fear as a protector. If we do not run when we see a snake, it would be an odd situation. The optimism that it will not harm you is highly misplaced. There should be appropriate fear in us to act as a protecting factor. The protection that fear bestows on us by making us take flight to avoid the situation is welcome for the physical well-being of the body. The emotional rush that it causes wears away in a little while, and the body returns to its normal condition. It is common to hear the expression, "my hands went cold with fear," when describing how you physically feel the signs of fear.

It is when the body does not return to normal after a certain period of time that the problem arises. The mind, by sending signals of the "physically non-existent, but dramatically persisting in the mind" situation prevents the body from coming back to normal. The mind and the body are now under the effect of the emotional fear. The person is "paralyzed by fear" figuratively. This person is far from being emotionally healthy, leave alone emotionally intelligent. He needs to understand the reason for the denial of his mind to accept the situation as done and get over with it.

What Happens When a Person is Overcome with Fear?

Believe me, your body will send signals to you that you cannot overlook, though the one small problem is that fear and anger produce much the same sort of bodily response. Why, even love (like fear) can make your heart beat faster!

What you would feel is something like this:

Your heart beats faster – and how!

You breathe faster.

The pupils of your eyes dilate. Can you recollect the posters of horror movies that depict this picture very graphically?

Perspiration increases. A very familiar sensation just before an interview or an examination is there.

The hair on the skin get erected causing "goose pimples."

This kind of heightened physical response prepares the body for the "fight or flight response."

How Does this Fear Affect Behaviour?

Let us take the instance of a student who fears examinations. At one level it can be a healthy fear that will spur him on to better preparation, and at another level, it can be an unhealthy fear that will make him desperate. He may resort to various malpractices. At what stage has the reasonable fear crossed over to the one that provokes unwanted action? It is quite possible that the insufficient preparation of the student to face the examination is the cause. And the cause of the insufficient preparation can be the lack of grasp of the subject by virtue of continuous absence or inadequate teaching, insufficient motivation, peer pressure of the wrong kind and sometimes an anti-social person. Unless the said student is literally shown the mirror to his fears, he may not be able to conquer them. The solutions are not instantaneous, but on the long term, this fear can be overcome by hitting at the root of the problem.

The executive who is unable to meet his targets has the fear of losing out on his chances for a better position and sometimes, on the job itself. He can on the one hand work more hours to meet the target, or on the other hand feel so stressed out that he takes recourse in escapist fare like alcohol and depression. Fear here is the cause of his stress or put another way, the fear of the consequences is the cause of the stress. This can turn out to be a vicious cycle unless deep introspection helps him to get at the root of the problem.

Then there is the fear of illness. The fear of the disease or the probability of the existence of the disease paralyzes some to the extent that they prefer not to know the diagnosis in factual terms. Unfortunately, this does not help them in any way except by pushing the disease from a treatable level to an untreatable one. Here, fear pushes the person into a state called "denial."

There are some who are trained to be "tough." In such people, weakness of any sort, as they perceive weakness, is something to fear! For example, a man who feels tears running down his cheeks fears that he is emotionally weak, because he has been conditioned to be "tough" and in that scheme of things, there is no place for tears. The same goes for an expected behaviour pattern like facing a thug. A man is expected to be brave and fight; if he is not, and runs from the situation, he is not measuring upto expectations – he is weak. It is a mindset, rather than the actual situation, which induces fear.

In all these instances, fear has hindered good decision-making and has caused adverse effects on the person physically and also in terms of emotional health. Sometimes it affects his interpersonal relationships in his family and immediate circle of society.

How to Conquer Fear

The first step in this exercise is to determine whether the fear is reasonable or is it too long drawn for the concerned event.

Then comes the next step of taking constructive action by facing the reality.

Getting to the question whether the fear is exceptionally long drawn? This simply means that the intensity of the fear gradually reduces in the mind, till it is but a vague memory that does not induce unpleasant thoughts in the mind, or a physical reaction like sweaty and cold hands and rapid heartbeat in the person. Initially, the fear may be gripping – and that is natural. For example in the case of a victim of a road accident, the person may be unwilling to ride the same vehicle after the initial phase of recovery from the injuries. The fear of being hit again remains till he summons the courage by rationalizing that accidents do not happen everyday to everyone. In

fact, it would be useful to point out that this was the first time for him. Once he overcomes the fear, say, by doing trial runs in the street during non-peak hours or any other tactic he might think of, he can summon the emotional strength to go on to the main road. He would have harnessed his emotional strength.

Then again, if you are the victim of a robbery, you are naturally afraid to stay alone in the house for some time. Slowly, it would be practical to look at solutions to prevent a robbery and steal yourself to face the situation. You begin by writing away your losses and overcoming depression about it, locking your doors extra carefully, employing or sharing a watchman with the neighbouring building, and also possibly by learning extra skills for self. Protection or simply keeping chilli powder at the door to fling on the assaulter. This chapter is not to help you build resolves in tackling burglars, but it is a common example that is incidental in most lives and illustrates how to build emotional competencies.

It is essential to understand the genesis and the outcome of fear (or in fact any other emotion) not only to enable the person to get over it, but to understand the fear/emotion another person is experiencing. In earlier chapters we have discussed that being emotionally healthy involves three levels, one in relation to the self, one to others and one to the society in general. Unless one has either personally undergone the same sort of trauma or have the capacity to understand the other person's pain, one cannot be termed emotionally intelligent. Simply put, he should be able to place himself in the other person's shoes and where necessary, help the other person with constructive suggestions.

There are times when these fears go overboard. When they persist over a great length of time and worse having intensified in degree become phobias. These can lead to various anxiety-prone problems and even depression. When this happens, we are not only losing out on emotional health, but also on the physical health. A simple example of a natural fear turning to a phobia or anxiety is when a person following a theft begins to repeatedly check the locks on his door—not once, not twice, but every half hour or so!

To check out whether someone is a victim of such uncalled for fears, try answering these questions.

1. How many times did you suffer from palpitations in the last month?
2. Did you spend the last six months worrying about things – more than the average person would?
3. Did you, in the last month, have persistent, senseless thoughts, impulses, images you cannot get out of your head?
4. In the past month did you get into the habit of repeatedly locking doors, arranging things, washing hands and so on?
5. In the past 2 months did you feel that others are staring at you while you are eating, speaking or attending meetings? In short, are others exceptionally interested in your activities?
6. In the past month, did you suffer from post-traumatic stress? For example, if you were the victim of a crime or accident and responded with fear, terror or utter helplessness at that time and are still reliving those memories after a couple of months, it may be that you are suffering from post-traumatic stress.
7. And last of all, to what extent have these incidences disrupted your normal life?

    - Not at all
    - Mildly
    - Moderately
    - To a large extent
    - Extremely

The answers to the questions are evident when you answer question number seven. The first two categories ('Not at all' and 'Mildly') are emotionally intelligent, the moderate one is moderately so, while people who come in the last two categories need to take stock of things to develop their EQ.

The following descriptions summarize the qualities of emotionally healthy adults:

- They are not fearful or anxious for more than a brief period of time.
- They will experience fear if physically threatened. (This is the natural fight/flight response.)
- They are able to confront and change their fear-causing beliefs to happier beliefs.
- They are often capable of appropriate action, despite high levels of fear.

While very few of us can hope to have satisfied all the criteria, it would be good to keep it as a long-term goal in our endeavour to better our EQ.

●●●

IX

Handling Anger

I was angry with my friend:
I told out my wrath, my wrath did end.
I was angry with my foe;
I told it not, my wrath did grow.

William Blake, (A Poison Tree)

Anger like fear, is a reaction to an event, which the mind perceives to be against our better interests. People are angry for all sorts of reasons, small and big, silly and serious. Some are angry for a long period of time, while others cool-off within minutes. Children are angry, and adults are angry. None are exempt from this emotion; the difference as always, lies in our capacity to handle our anger. To be able to do so it would be essential for us to recognize our reaction to the disturbing event that caused anger; then to assess whether we have got over our violent emotion in a short period of time. Or are we continuing to harbour anger for a protracted time?

Some facts about anger.

- Anger is a healthy emotion when expressed appropriately.
- Left unhandled it can destroy relationships, obstruct problem-solving skills and increase social withdrawal. Problematic interpersonal relationships may also disrupt employment because of interference in performance.
- Anger affects our physical health. It can tax our immune system, it can cause headaches and migraines, it can also cause

gastrointestinal symptoms, high Blood Pressure and Coronary Heart Disease.

- Anger is a healthy and valid emotion. It must be communicated in a healthy way. Some are taught not to express or show their anger. If stored or suppressed this could lead to frustration, and if expressed in a negative way it could create complicated problems.

What happens to the body when you are angry?

All of us have heard the phrase, 'shaking with anger'. That is what happens when one is extremely angry. The heart begins to violently pump blood into circulation and at a much faster rate. Our body reacts like a motor that is being overworked. It literally vibrates, and we begin to shake with rage.

You have also heard the phrase, 'red as a beetroot with anger'. Among those with a fair complexion, you can see the tell-tale red colouring spread on to cheeks giving a ruddy complexion. The blood that has been pumped into circulation goes mainly to the skin. Either or both of these circulatory changes can result in strokes and heart attacks!

From all of this, we can observe that anger is rather an aggressive emotion. It does produce some startling changes in our body. Does it seem worthwhile to have our body go through these extreme changes at the drop of a hat? While we cannot control the factors that make us angry, it is essential that we control our reaction to such situation.

By no stretch of imagination am I suggesting that we totally put a lid on anger. This would be worse than "blowing your top" as it would build up as a simmering emotion that has far-reaching effects on the person – health wise and personality wise.

What we need to learn is how to express our anger without having our body go through extreme changes. Many races are fairly adept at expressing it in simple plain language by verbally saying that they are upset/angry with your attitude, behaviour and so on. On the other hand, there are some races that prefer, in the name of courtesy, not to express their anger outwardly. In today's times, it would be difficult to advocate such tranquil behaviour patterns for everybody. There are some who say that exercises like Yoga and Transcendental Meditation help in achieving that state. For us ordinary humans, I would suggest deep breathing for a few minutes to let you "cool off" before taking any action. Count ten when you are angry, is one of those Grandma's tips that work wonders. Actually it takes about twenty minutes for the body to totally run out the changes produced in it by anger.

Let us take a closer look at some anger-patterns.

Psychologists say that anger is based upon some unfulfilled expectations. If you can let go of your expectations, you will not feel angry, or in other words, your expectations must be realistic. Some common examples of this sort of an anger are the teacher who is angry with the student for not doing his work, the manager who is angry with his junior for slip-short work, the husband who expects his wife to behave in a certain way that he considers appropriate, the person who is angry with the tailor for ruining his new suit and so on. Life offers many number of such instances. While they do make you angry, they are not really of the nature to have you "burst a blood vessel" for. Most marriages are replete with such a type of anger-examples. Each spouse expects the other to behave as per his/her expectations. It would be wise to appreciate one or more positive qualities of the other person and be focused on that. The total number of positive qualities that add up make for a better mental picture of the other person; besides, working together towards a common goal is a good remedy to rein in the wild expectations and thus keep the marriage on even keel.

There is also a type of anger connected with your disapproval of something or someone. This starts with the thought pattern "that should not be like this or that." Simple examples are those of not liking a political party, not liking your son's friends or daughter's choice of career, not liking this or that sect of people as what they do or don't do make you angry.

There is the type of anger that a subordinate staff-member cannot or will not vent on his superior. Perhaps we can call it the type that simmers in a person till it makes him stressed or makes him blow his top suddenly – the question of the final straw that broke the camel's back. Ravi, the young executive, was assigned a task. He had to complete it and hand over the estimates to the boss by that evening before going for a meeting. Ravi did all the work, but at the last minute, a distress call from another colleague to help out, delayed him by half an hour. The boss was extremely angry, and took him to task in the presence of quite a few people. Ravi tried to explain, the boss was not receptive to any explanation. However, Ravi was hurt and angry at the unfair treatment meted out to him.

He decides:

- To resign and find a new job.
- To meet the boss after he has cooled down and explain things to him

- Feels he has had enough, and decides to give it back to the boss in the same coin.
- Continues to work with the same superior without any explanation or clearing the air but all the time holding a grudge against him.
- Get drunk to went out his frustration in alcohol.

Explaining to his superior and clearing the air is possibly the best option. There are no guarantees that he would accept his explanation, but Ravi at least would have had the satisfaction of facing his anger and tackling it in an appropriate way. Eventually, he may well have to choose a different option, but he would have acted deliberately and not in anger. Running away from his extreme emotion by taking to negative ways like alcohol or giving way to depression can hardly be called constructive. This is the type of anger you "feel" but are at a loss to express. And resigning your job is definitely an overreaction.

However, even when you are silent, the way the body expresses itself by its posture – body language – is significant. The mouth is shut into a grim line, the fists are clenched; the jaw muscle contracting and relaxing alternately gives the face a mean and angry look, and the jaw itself that juts out, speaks of an aggressive attitude even while no words are used to express anger.

There is a type of anger that "keeps coming back" to you. This is a clear indication that the problem is not resolved. It means that your anger is off-target, or the wrong emotion is being expressed. Correctly expressed anger should not return. When it is returning, it could mean that one needs to introspect to find the cause/reason of that anger. Most often professional opinion is that such anger has its roots in childhood. The individual must face that childhood situation and accept it, however unpleasant and get over the anger/hatred caused by it, otherwise it would repeatedly come back to him.

Mr.Gopal is angry with his children for every little thing. He expects them to behave in a certain way, and any infringement sends him into rage. Sometimes, he picks on them without any valid reason. His anger keeps coming back. Finally, in a counselling session, it came to light that, during his childhood, his father, without provocation, constantly took him to task. He was scared to talk about it, leave alone protest; more so, as his father was a well-liked, and highly-respected man in the community as an understanding and gentle person. None would believe that he was such a ruthless task-master. Every occasion made Gopal more angry. He could neither talk about it without hurting his father's memory nor did he even feel that he was doing something wrong to his own children. His anger (at his father) kept coming back, and he expressed it in the only way he knew. Therapy helped him resolve the matter. Possibly, the whole question of repressed anger went back generations. In those times, it was a question of 'spare the rod and spoil the child!'

Current thinking is that most problems that deal with emotions, lie in a person's childhood. These childhood emotions have not found a channel of expression due to various reasons and simmer inside the person. The importance in encouraging a child and helping him by asking leading questions, helps him tackle his emotions by expressing them appropriately. If you see that a child is upset, it is advisable to open a channel of communication to find out what exactly happened and then label the feeling the child is experiencing: Once labelled that anger is directed against so and so, a small discussion can help the child in understanding the perspective of the other side, (isn't this what emotional intelligence is all about?) or a physical workout can temporarily put away anger till a more appropriate time is found to find rational answers.

Is your anger a reasonable emotion? Let us look at the questionnaire to arrive at a few conclusions.

1. Do you feel angry for no apparent reason?
2. Do you explode over little things?
3. Do you have unresolved anger?
4. Do you not understand where your anger comes from?
5. Do you want to direct your anger towards those around you?

6. Do you feel depressed or stressed most of the time?
7. Do you have high levels of anxiety or fear?

If you have answers with a 'yes' to any of these questions, it is advisable that you introspect and try to find answers to your unresolved issues.

How to get the better of anger

Having put your finger on the cause of your anger, the next step would be to find ways and means to learn how to get over your anger. For this:

- You must understand the roots of your anger.
- You must recognize your anger "style".
- You must release your anger in a safe and supportive environment. What are friends and family for?
- You must face and resolve the anger in you.
- You must reduce the high levels of stress and anxiety.

Emotionally healthy people should develop the following skills to be high on the score of EQ.

- They are comfortable with anger and hatred – their own and others.
- They do get angry when physically threatened.
- They do not get angry when verbally attacked.
- They are able to change their responses. This means that faced with an identical situation, they do not get angry.
- They get angry very rarely. Once they express their anger, it does not return.
- Do not dig up old arguments (this most often happens between angry couples in a marriage). The old anger is long gone. They are genuinely able to forgive.

"To err is human, to forgive is divine," is a common saying. Whole heartedly forgiving and forgetting past mistakes of another person requires more than simply uttering those words with the lips. No doubt, it is a good beginning, and provides a starting point to give up the anger as a spent emotion. But what it should be to an emotionally healthy person is the "end" of the unpleasant episode, never to intrude on the conscious mind again. And if ever, only as a lesson that this sort of anger has been previously experienced and done with. The lesson has been learnt.

Obviously, few of us achieve the above. Nevertheless, you will be happier if you are able to closely duplicate the above anger-responses of emotionally healthy adults. Let this be a long-term goal to achieve in the quest for a better Emotional Quotient.

•••

X

Overcoming Sadness

I sometimes hold in half a sin
To put in words the grief I feel;
For words, like Nature, half reveal
And half conceal the Soul within.

Tennyson (In Memoriam)

Who wants such an unpopular feeling?

YOU DO, if you want to be happy and emotionally intelligent.

This seems bizarre that I am saying that sadness can bring happiness, but it is true. Because in reality, everyone's life consists of unpleasant and sad moments along with the happy ones. Unless you are able to feel sadness and its accompaniments like grief, sobbing and tears, you will be forever avoiding sadness. Such avoidance makes one prone to addictive behaviour, psychosomatic symptoms, high levels of anxiety and a twisted or distorted reaction to the event. Sadness is a natural feeling, which if unfelt, remains as an unresolved trauma in our emotional lives. As with other emotions, feel it, and it will, with time, go away. Resist feeling it, and it hangs around for a long time. It will periodically erupt inappropriately in some other fashion because our body keeps trying every now and then to rid itself of this unwanted feeling.

How does one express sadness? Here again, there are levels of sadness. One is sad when a favourite friend leaves the town for another, one is sad when the result of an examination is not upto one's expectations, one is sad when one does not win a lottery, one is sad when one does not get the expected promotion or leaves a job, one is sad when one retires, one is sad when someone is sick in the family, and one is sad and grief stricken when a loved one passes away. One sees families breaking down when a daughter/ son leaves another town for a job. However, some other families might look upon the same occasion as a challenge and a part of growing up. There is no rule that says that everyone's sadness must be equal or proportionate, or that all sad things must be equally sad for all. Quite simply, this holds good for all emotions, but more so for sadness. Remember the old adage, laugh and the whole world laughs with you, but when you cry, you cry alone.

Some of the examples given are routine, and in fact mundane. These are the sort of things where the word "sad" is used loosely. To call some of the occasions cited above as disappointment with which the person is unable to cope with and a transient loss of a companionship due to unavoidable circumstances is probably more appropriate. Here coping skills such as reassessing the situation and keeping a perspective of the realities of the situation can work well to a person's advantage. Hence this may not be classed as sadness, or inconsolable grief. Then again, who is to say what hurts a person and makes him feel an emotion deeply? Possibly the occasions where such strong wrenching feelings happen are in the nature of the loss of a loved one or even loss of a person's entire live's possessions in fire, flood, theft, accident, riot, the loss of a job, the loss of a crop and so on.

All losses evoke what psychiatrists call the "grief process." The best way to maintain to emotional health after a loss is to allow yourself to feel the pain and share your sadness with safe and supportive people. This completes the full circle of the grief process and enables you to become free of it. Grief heals with time, and the greater the loss, the more the time required. Unfortunately, some people cut short the grief process, and they accumulate a lifetime of unresolved grief.

A person faced with loss typically goes through a series of stages of grief. Elizabeth Kubler-Ross described these changes when they occur in reaction to the losses of all sorts: the loss of a loved one, a pet, a job, a possession, money, a belief or anything a person cherishes. Adverse external circumstances can cause grief too, as in the case of a prolonged drought, the threat and fear of war, or financial disaster.

The stages of grief are:

- Denial – "No, it can't be!"
- Anger – "Why me! I don't deserve this!"
- Bargaining – "I'll do anything, just let this not happen."
- Depression – withdrawal, loss of hope.
- Acceptance – "It's alright. I can move on now."

All people do not go through the grief process in this sequence. There is much to-and-froing between stages more than once. If these feelings are repressed, they carry a heavy toll on the individual. The results may be chronic anxiety, tension, fear, confusion or shame.

The physical expression manifests itself in sleeplessness, body aches and pains or full-blown illness.

Tears give the much-wanted relief from this testing emotion. In the 50's it was unfashionable to cry. Negative judgments were commonly made about those who did so in public. Politicians for many years avoided anything even remotely connected to tears. 'Strong' and 'silent' were the watchword of the times. If so and so person breaks down, how will the rest of us learn to be brave? They have to draw courage from him! These were the words often used to describe the head of a family in bereavement, thereby placing an even further burden on him. He not only needs to suppress his tears, but needs to "be brave" for the sake of others! As if tears are a sign of weakness! On the other hand, they are a sign of strength. It does take strength and courage to allow all of one's emotions (particularly those that might be criticized) to be expressed. To be authentic emotionally shows more strength of character than to hide one's unpopular emotions. The person who cannot express the natural expression of tears and sobbing could on the other hand be termed emotionally crippled.

Fortunately, thanks to changing trends (and the visuals by the media) strong and silent is not the benchmark any more, but the caring and sharing person is! That is, today, a man is permitted his tears. Others will not disapprove. I am repeatedly harping on this point to drive home the fact that the role of "others approve or disapprove" cannot and should not govern our emotions. The concerned person should be wholly in charge. If he or she feels like crying (or laughing) he or she should feel free to do so; that would be the yardstick of a truly emotionally intelligent person.

There are still some who disapprove of almost any form of sadness, probably because they are afraid to feel it themselves. The phrase, "break down into tears," captures the essence of this disapproval. "Break down" somehow conjures a person totally losing control. While this is true in the initial and first phase of sadness when a person is in shock, it has a negative connotation. Slowly, with the perception of emotional intelligence on the increase, such stereotypes are being put to rest and men or women are taking the liberty of flowing with their emotions, even if it means a good cry.

Handling sadness in case of others is a difficult matter. Generally, one goes along with platitudes like, " Don't worry, time will heal everything." Time does heal nearly everything, but what is required is succour now, the ability to cope now, the strength to manage today. When a close friend or family member has gone through a sad experience, helping him to deal with it requires a lot of empathy. Most often, just being there, and going along with whatever he wants to do/say is a good idea. Enforced gaiety, or efforts to "get him out of his sadness" may be a trifle inappropriate. Friends and family do have a supportive role to play, and they should do it with a great deal of sensitivity.

A word about a special type of grief that happens when the after-effects of trauma last over a prolonged time – say over six months. This is called post-traumatic stress and is common among soldiers, victims of hijacking, kidnapping, and victims of violent crimes like rape. These people may repeatedly relive the experience and may be unable to concentrate or focus on current responsibilities; they are sometimes unresponsive to other people and sometimes overreact to minor disturbances. It may require therapy. In today's troubled times, it may be appropriate to be aware of such problems, for in no time in History has man been subjected to such uncalled for and unwarranted violence towards people totally unconcerned with the events in question.

Other Emotions

Guilt, surprisingly, is a useful emotion and keeps our behaviour in check. It tells us that we have crossed the boundaries, that we should not have and is a reminder from our conscience that we should act consistently with our values.

The extreme version of guilt is **shame.** While guilt arises from within, shame is imposed upon us from outside as a means of control—a tool used by parents and societies. Shame is communicated with a look, a tone of voice or with such words as, "shame on you." In contrast to guilt, shame can handicap a person's functioning and destroy his self-esteem. And to think that a child hears this numerous times from his well-wishers, his parents and teachers!

Another difference between both is that guilt separates the behaviour from the person; shame equates the behaviour with the person.

Guilt says, "What you did is bad, but you are acceptable."
Shame says, "What you did is bad, and you are bad."

An example. A student who failed in the exams because of irregular attendance and bunking classes for personal enjoyment, says to himself, "Next time, I will be regular, and save my freaking out for Sundays." This is appropriate guilt, but if he says, "I am a stupid worthless, failure, I do not deserve to pass," it is shame.
Here shame for the action becomes shame for the person.
An emotionally healthy person recognizes the difference between guilt and shame by disassociating the person from the act.

Skewed Emotions

These can otherwise be called "twisted emotions." These emotional responses happen all the time, and are hardly ever labelled as such. "Hurt feelings" that keep coming over and over again—guilt, jealousy or shame, that keep returning, are evidence that our emotions are blocked and we're unwilling to them. For adults, nearly all-adult anger directed towards spouses, children and neighbours is skewed. Likewise, tears that do not stop, and go on and on, are skewed.

A skewed discharge reduces our anxiety temporarily. And in keeping with a temporary solution to a problem, it does not hold good for long, and recurs – only to find solace in another skewed temporary emotion. I may not be far wrong if I say that most of the common responses to day-to-day issues are of a skewed pattern.

But why are so many skewed emotions expressed? The reason is that 97% of us learned in our growing-up years to "stuff" one or more of our emotions. Stuffed emotions are remembered by our bodies and our unconscious minds and act like internal irritants. (The popular word is that it ties up our insides into "knots.") They keep grating at us, causing anxiety and lead us to addictive situations in which we discharge our emotions in a skewed way.

How can you tell what is the truth behind the skewness? There are some tendencies that are useful to know.

If your sadness or anger is unresolved, the answer is likely to be in unresolved kid anger or sadness of childhood.

Skewed love starts in early youth, and is the result of absent or skewed parental expressions of love. We do use skewed love in the present to compensate for stuffed anger of our past.

We use guilt or shame to compensate for stuffed love in our past.

In short, we do use any emotion as skewed compensation of another.

The lengthy process of discovering and experiencing your own emotional truths will provide permanent relief. This does not imply that you will remain unhappy for much of that time. It does mean that there will be moments of difficulty, moments of stress, and moments of pain.

For maximum happiness, contentment and inner peace, we need all our emotions, not just the pleasant ones!

Emotionally healthy adults—

- Feel comfortable with sadness of their own and others.
- Allow their tears to flow.

- Feel good once their sobs and tears have been expressed.
- Are not stuck at recurring sadness, which happens when hatred is blocked, one's support system, either spiritually or otherwise, is insufficient and childhood hopelessness is being blocked.

The closer we get to the above, the happier we will be if we want to change some of our ideas about sadness. It is best to begin now.

●●●

XI

Assessing Yourself

Up to a point a man's life is shaped by environment, heredity, and movements and changes in the world about him. Then there comes a time when it lies within his grasp to shape the clay of his life into the sort of thing he wishes to be. Only the weak blame parents, their race, their times, lack of good fortune, or the quirks of fate. Everyone has it within his power to say, "This I am today; that I will be tomorrow."

Louis L'Amour

This test is a little more exhaustive than the one you took earlier in this book. In the interim, we have learnt how to tackle each emotion exhaustively. Many of the questions here are your perceptions of yourself and a few are your reactions to others. This is not a test where the score bestows you with a certain grade of emotional intelligence. You really cannot tell anyone that your EQ is so and so, and hence you are

a particularly gifted person. However, it will definitely reinforce your opinion of yourself, and guide you as to whether you are within acceptable limits, or it may suggest that you need to introspect, and go in for a major personality overhaul! It would be advisable to take this self-help test in one session, and try to complete it in thirty minutes. Moreover, this is only a self-help test, being honest with your answers is an important first step in the path of looking for improvement of your Emotional intelligence, and thereby rating yourself as a person with good EQ. Some of the situations may not be applicable to you, but imagine what your response would be if you were in that situation and mark your answer. I am sure you will come out with flying colours.

With these few guidelines under sections I, II & III, get, set and go!

Section I

1. Though there is some scope for improvement, I like myself as I am
   (a) Agree
   (b) Partially Agree
   (c) Disagree

2. When I get into a work mood, I feel strong, capable and competent
   (a) Often
   (b) Sometimes
   (c) Almost never

3. I can pin-point exactly what aspect of the problem is troubling me
   (a) Often
   (b) Sometimes
   (c) Rarely

4. I do my best even if nobody sees it
   (a) Often

(b) Sometimes

(c) Almost never

5. I enjoy spending time with my friends
   (a) Often
   (b) Sometimes
   (c) Almost never

6. I pay compliments to people when they deserve them
   (a) Often
   (b) Sometimes
   (c) Almost never

7. I finish the work that I begin
   (a) Often
   (b) Sometimes
   (c) Almost never

8. I have a need to make a difference (to leave a lasting impression)
   (a) Often
   (b) Sometimes
   (c) Almost never

9. It is better to remain distant and neutral until you really know a person
   (a) Often
   (b) Sometimes
   (c) Almost never

10. When someone does me a favour without being asked, I wonder what is they want from me
    (a) Mostly true
    (b) Somewhat true
    (c) Not true

11. People who are emotional, that is people who get worked-up make me uncomfortable

(a) Mostly true
(b) Somewhat true
(c) Not true

12. When I hear about some else's problem, I can think of many solutions
    (a) Often
    (b) Sometimes
    (c) Rarely

13. I have confidence in my abilities
    (a) Much
    (b) Somewhat
    (c) Little

14. When I deviate from standard procedures, I feel
    (a) Comfortable
    (b) Somewhat uncomfortable
    (c) Totally uncomfortable

15. I am unhappy for reasons that I cannot understand
    (a) Rarely
    (b) Sometimes
    (c) Often

16. When there is something unpleasant to do
    (a) I do it immediately
    (b) Postpone it till I cannot avoid it any longer
    (c) Find somebody else to do it for me

17. In my view, happiness depends on
    (a) The way one leads one's life
    (b) One's environment
    (c) One's luck

18. In my workplace, I know what is happening around me
    (a) Always well aware

(b) Don't pay much attention
(c) Not bothered

19. When I am upset while dealing with a rude Government official, I
   (a) Step back and reassess the situation
   (b) Take it out on someone
   (c) Start doing things that I later regret

20. When I break a rule,
   (a) I feel bad, but get over it quickly
   (b) I don't allow myself to feel bad
   (c) I really don't care

21. I get motivated when I
   (a) Picture the expected outcome and then do my best to achieve it
   (b) Ignore the possible outcome and do what needs to be done
   (c) Picture the worst possible outcome and then do my best to avoid it

22. Sizing up people's character is
   (a) Something I'm good at
   (b) One of my weakest points
   (c) Something I never attempted

23. When I fail in something it is usually due to
   (a) Lack of preparation and efforts on my part
   (b) Lack of ability on my part
   (c) External factors i.e. things that have nothing to do with me like unreasonably difficult task, improper help etc

24. I talk about my most intimate issues and private feelings to anybody and everybody
   (a) I discuss only with family members and friends
   (b) I do so but it may be inappropriate

(c) Personal problems should remain personal

25. When I have to communicate my positive feelings to someone, I
    (a) Do something nice, write or say it to that person
    (b) Tell it to someone else, so that the message will eventually reach him
    (c) Keep it to myself so as not to spoil that person by too much praise.

26. My relationship with friends is
    (a) I make acquaintances easily but take some time to make a good friend
    (b) I make acquaintances with some difficulties and take a very long time to make a friend
    (c) I am distrustful for a long time before I open up

27. What is the best time for revealing some shocking news to your family
    (a) When the family is generally in good times
    (b) As soon as possible irrespective of circumstances
    (c) When the family is already in trouble - after all how does one more problem matter?

28. When I am upset
    (a) I can tell exactly how I feel - sad, lonely, angry etc
    (b) I can usually tell but sometimes it is difficult to identify the reason exactly
    (c) I cannot tell what I am feeling

29. When I have a major problem that I am finding very difficult to deal
    (a) I will deal with it myself
    (b) I will go to my friends for advice and support
    (c) I will pretend it does not exit.

Section II

1. I say things that I regret later
   (a) Often
   (b) Sometimes
   (c) Rarely

2. When I see something that I like or want, I cannot be at peace till I get it
   (a) Often
   (b) Sometimes
   (c) Rarely

3. I'm ashamed about how I look and behave
   (a) Often

(b) Sometimes
(c) Rarely

4. I'm uneasy in situations where I am expected to display affection
   (a) Often
   (b) Sometimes
   (c) Rarely

5. I feel uncomfortable when I hug someone other than my family members
   (a) Often
   (b) Sometimes
   (c) Rarely

6. When I feel irritated I know what or who is upsetting me
   (a) Often
   (b) Sometimes
   (c) Rarely

7. I buy things that I can't really afford
   (a) Often
   (b) Sometimes
   (c) Rarely

8. Even when I do my best I feel guilty that some things could not be done
   (a) Often
   (b) Sometimes
   (c) Rarely

9. I feel like calling myself self-depreciating names like stupid, loser etc
   (a) Often
   (b) Sometimes
   (c) Rarely

10. People have problems but I have so many that I cannot tolerate them
   (a) Often
   (b) Sometimes
   (c) Rarely

11. People make me feel bad about myself
   (a) Often
   (b) Sometimes
   (c) Rarely

12. I panic when I have to face someone who is angry
   (a) Often
   (b) Sometimes
   (c) Rarely

13. When I want to do something, I run into obstacles which prevent me from reaching my goals
   (a) Often
   (b) Sometimes
   (c) Rarely

14. I cannot stop thinking about my problems
   (a) Often
   (b) Sometimes
   (c) Rarely

15. I will do everything I can to prevent myself from crying
   (a) Often
   (b) Sometimes
   (c) Rarely

16. I cannot get over the guilt over the small mistakes that I often make
   (a) Mostly true

(b) Somewhat true
(c) Not true

17. I am bored
(a) Often
(b) Sometimes
(c) Rarely

18. I worry about things that other people don't even think about
(a) Often
(b) Sometimes
(c) Rarely

19. I have difficulty in saying things like - 'I like you,' even when I really like a person
(a) Often
(b) Sometimes
(c) Rarely

20. My life is full of dead ends
(a) Mostly true
(b) Somewhat true
(c) Not true

21. I need someone to push me to start anything
(a) Often
(b) Sometimes
(c) Rarely

22. I'm not satisfied with my work unless someone praises it
(a) Mostly true
(b) Sometimes true
(c) Not true

23. People tell me I overreact to minor problems
(a) Often

(b) Sometimes

(c) Rarely

24. I do what people expect me to do even when I disagree with them
    (a) Often
    (b) Sometimes
    (c) Rarely

25. No matter how much I complete, I feel I should have done more
    (a) Often
    (b) Sometimes
    (c) Rarely

26. Does gut feeling play a role in your decisions?
    (a) Absolutely no bearing
    (b) Very little bearing
    (c) Considerable weightage

27. When a new prospect comes up
    (a) I don't expect much so that I don't get disappointed later
    (b) I have no pre-conceived notions, I take it as it comes
    (c) I expect the best, and I prefer to deal with problems as they arise

28. When someone shouts at me
    (a) I get very upset
    (b) I let it go without confronting the person
    (c) I confront the person and ask for reasons

29. When I get frustrated
    (a) I stop what I am doing and use my time for something else more productively
    (b) I persist and complete the task
    (c) I take a break, and continue with the task

30. In general, it is best

   (a) Not to set goals and just go with the flow
   (b) To set goals that are not too challenging and easy to achieve
   (c) To set goals that are challenging but possible to achieve.

Section III

1. Mrs. Pavitra is a successful doctor and is well liked by everyone. Every time she goes to a family gathering, she talks only about her children or her practice. The reason she does not participate in any other topic is

   (a) Her belief that everybody finds these topics interesting
   (b) Her wish to keep the conversation to neutral topics
   (c) Her wish to keep the conversation in her area of expertise.

2. Mr. Suri, 39, has a weight problem. He has tried various diets and exercise programmes, but never really continued with them. On the verge of middle age, he is highly motivated after hearing about his friend's heart attack and is determined to lose weight. Which strategy would you suggest?

   (a) An easy programme that requires very little will power
   (b) A regular diet with light exercise
   (c) Strict diet and heavy exercise that will require a lot of will power.

3. Mr. Prem is a capable lecturer but has a difficult personality. He gets along with his professors but confines strictly to his job description. He is tough with his students, keeps them waiting and is very critical. The reason for this behaviour is

   (a) He is an unpredictable and irrational person
   (b) He had previous bad experiences and prefers to keep students in their place
   (c) He has a poor opinion about the quality of today's education.

4. For you, as a new student, what is the best way to get along with Mr. Prem?

a. Show him how smart you are
b. Treat him with respect without becoming friendly
c. Engage him in a discussion of his views on education

5. You have an opportunity to work on an important project that can get you a promotion. You have spent a lot of time and effort. Unfortunately you come third. What do you do?
   a. Find reasons to believe that the selection was not fair
   b. Have a look at the winner's proposal and learn how it was better than yours
   c. Forget the sad story and go on with your life.

6. Once again your marriage proposal did not come through. How do you react?
   a. I will accept the next proposal and change the person into whom I want him/her to be
   b. I will remain optimistic and find the right person
   c. I will give up on this temporarily and concentrate on my career.

7. Your best friend's grandmother died a month ago. They were very close and your friend is very sad. Do you
   a. Take your friend to a tragedy cinema
   b. Tell him about your own problems to take his mind off his grief
   c. Be around and be available.

8. Speaking out about negative emotions is
   a. Always unhealthy, whatever the circumstances
   b. Generally healthy but inappropriate in some circumstances
   c. Generally healthy but inappropriate in some circumstances.

9. You are in the middle of a heated argument with your husband/wife. You are about to say something very nasty that will hurt further. The best way to deal with the situation is
   a. Just walk away
   b. Let the anger burst out because it is unhealthy to bottle up emotions and apologize later

c. Say that you are too angry, stop for a while and resolve your differences.

10. You are a part of a group working together on a project; you are trying to solve a special problem with a creative approach. So far, no solutions are within sight. You are stuck. The best way to go about it is

    a. Put pressure on the group by telling them it is not a joke and they must find an answer

    b. Take turns in making suggestions

    c. Go through the solutions of past problems in search of inspiration.

That was easy. Wasn't it? All you had to do was to answer some questions about how you feel about yourself, and how you feel about certain events. While completing the points each of you scored, various aspects like your traits, your adaptability, that is, your capacity to bounce back from problematic situations, your capacity to communicate and interact with others, and most important of all, whether you are comfortable with yourself, and whether you have a true perspective of your talents and weaknesses come to therefore.

Now we come to the score.

Sec. I. In this part, "a" gets 3 points,

"b" gets 1 point

and "c" gets none.

Sec. II. In this part, "c" gets 3 points

"b" gets 1 point

and "a" gets none.

Sec. III. In this part, "a" gets 1 point

and "b" or "c" gets 2 points.

The total score adds up to 200 points.

Researchers claim that 144 is as high as one can go, and 37 is the lowest possible. The average is 100.

If you have scored anything more than 100, your report for a real test on EQ under observation would read like this. (This was a rehearsal.)

"Your Emotional IQ is very good – higher than the average. This means that, in general you express your feelings directly and with good timing. You are optimistic and positive, and adapt well to changed circumstances. You deal effectively with stress, interact and communicate adequately. You are comfortable with yourself; you know and appreciate your talents and strong points as well as your weaknesses."

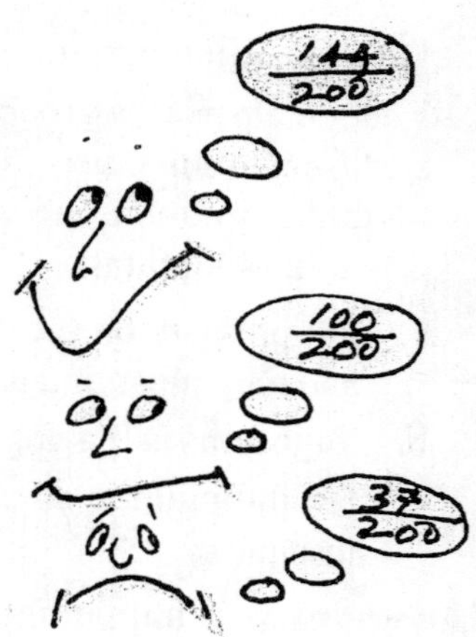

If your score unfortunately were much lower than 100, say around fifty or sixty, it would read like this:

"The bad news is your Emotional IQ is quite low. Practically this means that you are not taking full advantage of your potential, whatever that might be. Low EIQ has a negative impact on all aspects of your life – from relationships (you might be viewed by others as a critical, inexpressive, inhibited, detached, cold, rigid and blame-shifting person), emotional health (you might be prone to anxiety, depression, excessive guilt, aggressiveness, low self-respect, stress-related problems) to your motivation, creativity, ability to bounce back, resilience and persistence."

For everyone, whatever your score might be – it can only make you better. There is room for improvement. The good news is that you can do something about it by starting right now. Start with identifying your problem areas. Paying attention to your interactions with other people and to yourself is a good launching point, as is asking your friends and spouse as to what bothers them about your behaviour. Try to really listen, without being judgmental and defensive. Read books on self-improvement. You will be amazed to find how good, strong and happy you feel.

As the Nike ad says, 'Go Get It!'

•••

XII

The Complete Man

This word is a happening word in today's society and perhaps nothing symbolizes a man with good EIQ more than this phrase.

In all the previous chapters we have been working towards that goal and have successfully achieved:

- The capability to recognize and label our feelings and needs, reconcile them with our long-term goals and with the needs and feelings of other people involved.

We now need to cultivate

- The ability to identify ways of meeting our goals and needs and to soothe our feelings.
- Then we need to motivate ourselves and mobilize all our internal resources like energy, effort, discipline, perseverance and resilience.
- External resources like building social networks through effective communication, social insight, empathy, reading other's emotions and setting boundaries.

How to Meet Our Goals

The answer is simple! By having our goals reasonably within reach. Once you have reached that goal, then it is time to shift that goal a little further and then work towards it.

It was the great prophet, Paul who said, "This one thing I do." In unmistakable terms he stated that his life was to have a singleness of purpose. One thing, he would do!

"This day we sailed forward," were the simple words Columbus wrote in his book each day. How definite, how determined to do one thing! The crew may rebel, storms might come, but he had a single objective. Nothing was to interfere. And with that objective a new world was discovered and the history of mankind was changed. So set your goals at a level where you can stretch yourself a little, and then, one arm's length at a time, climb to your full potential.

In pursuit of these goals, there will be some pitfalls and some pain. It is in you to get up, dust yourself, smile and get on with it. Sometimes, there may be some tears, and with the help of a friend, or life partner, wipe them away, and get along with the job. We soothe our hurt feelings perhaps with a wit and perhaps with a shrug that says, "This too will pass," and move on to finish the one thing you started out to do.

In this quest, a vital factor is motivation. This can be from within, fuelling the desire to succeed with energy, effort, discipline, perseverance and resilience. There is a sign in a General Motors Corporation plant that apparently says this:

"According to the theory of aerodynamics, as may be readily demonstrated through wind-tunnel experiments, the bumble-bee is unable to fly. This is because its size, weight and shape of the body in relation to the wing-spread, make flying impossible."

But the bumble-bee, being ignorant of these scientific facts, goes ahead and flies anyway—and makes a little honey in the process too!

My guess is that the bumble-bee was highly motivated, (possibly its very survival depended on it) used its energy, asserted the harshest of discipline and persevered in its flight with the resilience of, well a bumble-bee. In the end, it wins its pot of gold too as you will in your quest for your pot of the figurative gold.

While the bee achieved all this on its own, today, you can and will take some help from other sources external to yourself. You will communicate with colleagues and friends and family too in such a way that there is harmony. You will attempt to understand their feelings and concerns, and you will learn yourself to set boundaries that you will respect. You have learnt to live by your values, and that is perhaps your biggest victory.

Not to forget that endearing quality that makes up for misgivings here and there. Let me tell you a small story. Many years ago some friends were discussing the suitability of Calvin Coolidge as a presidential candidate. Some disagreed, arguing that he was too quiet, lacked colour and political personality. "No one would like him," objected one in the group.

One little girl piped in: "I like Mr. Coolidge." Then she displayed a finger with a bandage on it. "He was the only one who asked me about my sore finger."

Sounds familiar? You guessed right. That is the complete man!

Portrait of the Complete Man

- Maintains high self-esteem; is willing to attempt new learning and behaviour patterns and is able to handle setbacks without loss of self-esteem.
- Monitors emotions, managing and expressing them appropriately.
- Recognizes potential emotional problems in self and others and seeks help when appropriate.
- Feels that life has meaning. Lives by cherished values.
- Manages stress with skill and enjoyment, not letting it overwhelm him.
- Cultivates physical fitness.
- Develops supportive friendships; can socialize with others without being influenced by alcohol and other drugs.

- Can develop and maintain intimacy with another in a successful long-term partnership like marriage.
- Trusts and relies on a power greater than self.
- Continues growing, learning and facing new challenges with each advancing year.

Do more than exist, live
Do more than touch, feel
Do more than look, observe
Do more than read, absorb
Do more than hear, listen
Do more than listen, understand
Do more than think, ponder
Do more than talk, say something
Do more than say, DO something
Become the complete person!

Is all wisdom and teaching nothing saving a collection of platitudes? Take fifty of our current proverbial sayings—they are so trite, so threadbare. Nonetheless, they embody the concentrated experience of the race and the man who orders his life according to their teaching, cannot go wrong. How easy it all seems! But has anyone ever done so? Never.

Has any man ever attained inner harmony and a total understanding of his emotions by pondering the experience of others? Not since the world began.

He must pass through fire!

You have taken on the challenging duty of evaluating yourself time and again while turning the pages of this book.

You have asked yourself some probing questions and searched for answers in the depths of your mind.

You have not spared any effort to delve into the depths of your heart to explore your emotions.

You have gone through the semifinals and come out unscathed, if a trifle confused about some unanswered questions.

Then began the deeper exploration of each single emotion you have felt. You have analyzed your love and your laughter, your sorrow and your tears, your shame and your guilt at length.

You took in your stride the churned emotions all this introspection has caused and treated it as a process of catharsis.

You took the final test that was exhaustive in its content and have emerged

THE WINNER!

YOU ARE THE COMPLETE MAN!

CONGRATULATIONS!

•••